Winter and Summer

HOUGHTON MIFFLIN

BOSTON

Maya did NOT like winter.
It was too cold!

1

Then Maya's best friend,
Beth, moved to California.

"It's so hot here! I can't
sled or skate," Beth said.
"You're lucky to have cold
weather."

Beth was right! Maya put on
her coat and ran outside.

Insight Phrase Book
Spanish
Original text: Elisabeth Graf-Riemann
Editor: Sabine von Loeffelholz
English edition translated by: Paul Fletcher
Edited by: Renée Holler and Sylvia Suddes

Managing Editor: Tony Halliday
Editorial Director: Brian Bell

CONTACTING THE EDITORS: As every effort is made to provide accurate information in this publication, we would appreciate it if readers would call our attention to any errors and omissions by contacting:
Apa Publications, PO Box 7910, London SE1 1WE, England.
Fax: (44 20) 7403 0290
e-mail: insight@apaguide.demon.co.uk

Information has been obtained from sources believed to be reliable,
but its accuracy and completeness, and the opinions based thereon,
are not guaranteed.

© 2002 APA Publications GmbH & Co. Verlag KG Singapore Branch, Singapore.

1st edition 2000, updated 2002

Printed in Singapore by Insight Print Serveices (Pte) Ltd

Original edition © Polyglott-Verlag Dr Bolte KG, Munich

Distributed in the UK & Ireland by:
GeoCenter International Ltd
The Viables Centre, Harrow Way, Basingstoke,
Hampshire RG22 4BJ
Tel: (44 1256) 817987, Fax: (44 1256) 817-988

Distributed in the United States by:
Langenscheidt Publishers, Inc.
46–35 54th Road, Maspeth, NY 11378
Tel: (1 718) 784-0055, Fax: (1 718) 784-0640

Worldwide distribution enquiries:
APA Publications GmbH & Co. Verlag KG (Singapore Branch)
38 Joo Koon Road, Singapore 628990
Tel: (65) 865-1600, Fax: (65) 861-6438

INSIGHT PHRASE BOOK
SPANISH

APA PUBLICATIONS
Part of the Langenscheidt Publishing Group

L

Contents

Introduction

About this book

Insight Phrase Books are the perfect companion when touring abroad as they cover all the everyday situations faced by travellers who are not familiar with the language of their holiday hosts.

The sentences and expressions translated here have been chosen carefully so that you can make yourself understood quickly and easily. You will not find any complicated sentence constructions or long word lists. Nearly all the sentences have been compiled from basic phrases so that by substituting words and other expressions, you will be able to cope with a variety of conversational situations.

The word lists at the end of each section are themed and this will make it easy for you to vary what you want to say. You will be able to make yourself understood quickly in Spanish with the minimum vocabulary. You won't need to spend a long time searching for the word you want.

So that you can understand what others are saying to you in everyday situations, for example at the doctors, at the border, we have marked with an asterisk (*) those phrases and questions that you are likely to hear frequently.

The simplified pronunciation guide geared towards English speakers will help you to say the words you need in a recognisable manner. There is a summary of basic pronunciation, together with a brief introduction to Spanish grammar.

This introduction is followed by nine chapters containing examples of sentences from general and tourist-related situations. You will find general tips and guidance not just in the chapter entitled Practical Information, but also elsewhere in the book. The various feature boxes contain useful information on such matters as meal times, using public transport and telephones, the different categories of hotels and restaurants and lots more.

At the end of the book you will find an English-Spanish dictionary, which can be used for reference and as an index – the page number refers to an entry in one of the nine chapters. The Spanish-English dictionary contains a selection of important words and abbreviations, which you are likely to encounter on signs, notices and information boards.

Hoping you have lots of fun on your travels, ¡Buen viaje! [b**wen bee-a**khay] *(Have a good trip!)*

Pronunciation

Spanish is actually an easy language to speak as the written word follows consistent rules. After a while you may not need to use the pronunciation guide. Please read the section below entitled Stress and Accented Letters. Our guide to pronunciation always shows the stressed syllable in bold type, e.g. momento [mo**mayn**to] (moment), mesa [**may**sa] (table).

Certain letters can cause confusion to the English speaker, e.g. **c** before **e** or **i** and **z** before **a**, **o** or **u** produce **th**, as in thin, e.g. cinco [**theen**ko] (five). The Spanish that is spoken in Latin America, the US and the Canary Islands does not recognise this sound. Here **s**, **z** and **c** followed by **e** or **i** are always pronounced as **s**.

Another difference that puzzles English speakers is the Spanish **v**, which often sounds like a **b**, as in vino [**bee**no] (wine). The **b** is always pronounced exactly the same as an English **b**, as in bargain.

Other important pronunciation points:

- c is pronounced as a k before a, o, u, e.g. cama [kama] *(bed)*, before e and i as a th, e.g. cinco [theenko] *(five)*

- ch is always pronounced as ch as in chair, e.g. muchacho [muchacho] *(boy)*

- e is pronounced as ay, but flatter and with less emphasis on the y

- eu is pronounced as two sounds, e.g. Europa [e-uropa] *(Europe)*

- g before a, o and u is pronounced as a hard g, e.g. gol [gol] *(goal)*, before e and i as a soft g, e.g. gente [khayntay] *(people)*

- h is always silent, e.g. hotel [otayl] *(hotel)*

- j is similar to the soft g, e.g. jarra [kharra] *(jug)*

- ll is pronounced like the y in yoghurt, e.g. llegar [yaygar] *(arrive)*, gallo [gayo] *(cock, rooster)*

- ñ is pronounced ny, e.g. España [espanya] *(Spain)*

- qu is like k, e.g. queso [kayso] *(cheese)*

- r is rolled with the tongue, especially at the beginning of a word, e.g. roto [roto] *(broken)* rr is rolled even more

- s is always soft, e.g. sábado [sabado] *(Saturday)*

- z becomes a th sound, e.g. zumo [thoomo] *(juice)*

- the tie (‿) indicates when words are slurred together, e.g. por aquí [por‿aki] *(near here)*.

Stress and accented letters

When we pronounce a word, we give special force to a syllable and pronounce the vowel sound louder. In Spanish, like in English, the stress is important because it can indicate different meanings, for example, papa [papa] *(potato)*, papá [papa] *(dad)*. The accent above the a in

papá indicates that this syllable is stressed. When no syllable is accented, then these rules apply:

Where words end with a vowel or end with an n or an s, then it is the syllable before last which is emphasised, e.g. banco [banko] *(bank)*, todos [todos] *(all)*. It is the final syllable which is stressed where words end in a consonant (apart from n and s), e.g. profesor [profaysor] *(teacher)*, Madrid [madrid] *(Madrid)*.

The acute accent which appears on certain words does not, as in French and German, change the pronunciation of a vowel, but shows which syllable is stressed, in cases where the emphasis does not conform with the usual rules described above. The accented vowel is always stressed, e.g. música [moosika] *(music)*.

One-syllable words do not have a marked accent, except to distinguish between words which are spelt in the same way, e.g. dé [day] (give), de [day] (of); el [el] (the), él [el] (he).

Punctuation

Two unique features of written Spanish are the inverted question mark and exclamation mark. The inverted form is placed at the beginning of the question or exclamation, e.g. ¿Dónde? [donday] *(where?)*, ¡Olé! [olay] *(bravo!)*

The Spanish alphabet

A a	[a]	N n	[aynay]
B b	[bay]	Ñ ñ	[aynyay]
C c	[thay]	O o	[o]
Ch ch	[chay]	P p	[pay]
D d	[day]	Q q	[koo]
E e	[ay]	R r	[ayray]
F f	[ayfay]	S s	[aysay]
G g	[khay]	T t	[tay]
H h	[achay]	U u	[oo]
I i	[ee]	V v	[oovay]
J j	[khota]	W w	[oobay doblay]
K k	[ka]	X x	[aykees]
L l	[aylay]	Y y	[ee greeayga]
Ll ll	[aylyay]	Z z	[thayta]
M m	[aymay]		

Spanish Grammar In Brief

The article

In Spanish all nouns are either masculine *(m)* or feminine *(f)*.

The definite article

Masculine singular:
el coche [el **ko**chay] *(the car)*

Masculine plural:
los coches [los **ko**chays] *(the cars)*

Feminine singular:
la cama [la **ka**ma] *(the bed)*

Feminine plural:
las camas [las **ka**mas] *(the beds)*

Indefinite article

Masculine singular:
un coche [oon **ko**chay] *(a car)*

Masculine plural:
unos coches [**oo**nos **ko**chays] *(some cars)*

Feminine singular:
una cama [**oo**na **ka**ma] *(a bed)*

Feminine plural:
unas camas [**oo**nas **ka**mas] *(some beds)*

Unos/unas means some. Beds is simply camas and is not preceded by an article.

Nouns

Masculine nouns usually end in -o, e.g. el metro [el **may**tro] *(the underground)*, feminine nouns in -a, e.g. la mañana [la man**yan**a] *(tomorrow)*.

There are a few **exceptions** to this rule, e.g. el día [el **dee**a] *(the day)*; la radio [la **ra**deeo] *(the radio)*.

Nouns which end in -e can be either masculine or feminine, e.g. el hombre [el␣**om**bray] *(man)*; la noche [la **no**chay] *(the night/the evening)*.

Nouns ending in -or are masculine, e.g. el profesor [el profe**sor**] *(the teacher)*.

Nouns ending in -**ción** or -**ad** are feminine, e.g. la reducción [la redook**theeon**] *(discount)*; la mitad [la mee**tad**] *(the half)*.

Adding an -a or replacing an -o with an -a often creates the feminine form of a noun, e.g. el novio [el **no**beeo], la novia [la **no**beea] *(boyfriend/girlfriend)*.

Forming plurals

Nouns which end in a vowel form their plural by adding -s, e.g. el año [el **an**yo]/los años [los **an**yos] *(the year/the years)*; la calle [la **ka**-yay]/las calles [las **ka**-yays] *(the street/the streets)*.

Nouns ending in a consonant add -**es** to form the plural, e.g. el doctor [el dok**tor**]/los doctores [los dok**to**rays] *(the doctor/the doctors)*; la pensión [la pen**syon**]/las pensiones [las pen**syon**ays] *(guesthouse/guesthouses)*.

Adjectives

Most Spanish adjectives end like nouns with -o *(m)* and -a *(f)*, the plurals being -os/-as), e.g. bueno/buena [**bwayn**o/**bwayn**a] *(good)*; caro/cara [**karo**/**kara**] *(dear, expensive)*.

The adjective ending always matches the noun, i.e. masculine/feminine, singular/plural, e.g. una comida buena [**oo**na ko**mee**da **bwayn**a] *(a good meal)*; la comida es buena [la ko**mee**da ays **bwayn**a] *(The meal is good)*.

Adjectives ending in -e, -l, -z etc. do not usually have their own feminine form, e.g. grande [**gran**day] *(large)*; azul [a**thool**] *(blue)*; feliz [fe**leeth**] *(happy)*.

Adjectives indicating a nationality always use the feminine form, e.g. inglés [een**glays**] – inglesa [een**glay**sa] *(English [language] – English [person])*, español [ayspan**yol**] – española [ayspan**yola**] *(Spanish [language] – Spanish [person])*.

Position of the adjective

The adjective normally follows the noun, e.g. la casa grande [la **ca**sa **gran**day] *(the large house)*.

With expressions of quantity (many, few, etc.), or to give extra emphasis, the adjective can precede the noun, e.g. muchos coches [**moo**chos **ko**chays] *(many cars)*.

Comparison of adjectives

To create the comparative form, the word más (more) precedes the adjective, e.g. caro [**ka**ro] *(dear)* – más caro [mas **ka**ro] *(more expensive)*. To form the superlative, más is preceded by the definite article, e.g. el más caro [el mas **ka**ro] *(the most expensive)*. Direct comparisons are created with que, e.g. más caro que [mas **ka**ro kay] *(more expensive than)*.

Some commonly used adjectives do not fit into the pattern, e.g. bueno [**bway**no] *(good)*, mejor [may**khor**] *(better)*; malo [**ma**lo] *(bad)*, peor [pay**or**] *(worse)*; grande [**gran**day] *(large)*, mayor [may**or**] *(larger)*; pequeño [pay**kay**nyo] *(small)*, menor [may**nor**] *(smaller)*.

Adverbs

The adverb is formed from the feminine form of the adjective by adding -**mente**, e.g. claro [**kla**ro] – claramente [klara**men**tay] *(clearly)*.

Irregular adverbs are bien [byen] *(well)* and mal [mal] *(badly)*, e.g. Está bien. [ay**sta** bee-**ayn**] *(It's OK)*; Estoy mal. [ay**stoy** mal] *(I'm not well)*.

Pronouns

Subject pronouns

yo [yo] *(I)*
tú [too] *(you [singular/familiar])*
él [el] (he); ella [**ey**a] *(she)*; usted [oos**tay**] *(you [singular/formal])*
nosotros/nosotras [no**so**tros/no**so**tras] *(we)*
vosotros/vosotras [vo**so**tros/vo**so**tras] *(you [plural/familiar])*
ellos [**ay**-os] *(they [masculine])*; ellas [**ay**-as] *(they [feminine])*; ustedes [oos**tay**days] *(you [plural/formal])*

Object pronouns

me [may] *(me, to me)*
te [tay] *(you, to you [singular/familiar])*

le [lay] *(to him, to her, to you [singular/formal])*
lo/la [lo/la] *(him, her, you [singular/formal])*
nos [nos] *(us, to us)*
os [os] *(you, to you [familiar/plural])*
les [les] *(to them, to you [plural/formal])*
los/las [los/las] *(them, you [plural/formal])*

Possessive pronouns

mi [mee] *(my)*
tu [too] *(your [singular/familiar])*
su [soo] *(his, her, your [singular/formal])*
nuestro/nuestra [**nooays**tro/**nooays**tra] *(our)*
vuestro/vuestra [**vooays**tro/**vooays**tra] *(your [plural/familiar])*
su [soo] *(their, your [plural/formal])*

In all of the above cases, the plural is formed by adding an -s, e.g. mis cheques [mees **chay**kays] *(my cheques)*.

Demonstrative pronouns

Singular: este *(m)* [**ays**tay], esta *(f)* [**ays**ta] *(this one [near me])*; este garaje [**ays**tay ga**rak**hay] *(this garage)*

Plural: estos/estas [**ays**tos/**ays**tas] *(these [near me])*

Singular: ese *(m)* [**ays**say], esa *(f)* [**ays**sa] *(that one [near you])*

Plural: esos/esas [**ays**sos/**ays**sas] *(those [near you])*

Singular: aquel *(m)* [a**kayl**], aquella *(f)* [a**kay**-a] *(that one [over there])*

Plural: aquellos/aquellas [a**kay**-os/a**kay**-as] *(those [over there])*

Demonstrative pronouns can be used without nouns: esto [**ays**to] *(this here)* – eso [**ays**so] *(that there)* – aquello [a**kay**-o] *(that one over there)*; ¿Qué es esto? [kay_ays **ays**to] *(What is this?)*

Prepositions

en [en] *(in, by*
a [a] *(to)*
de [day] *(from)*

para [**pa**ra] *(for)*
por [por] *(for, per)*
con [kon] *(with)*
sin [seen] *(without)*
entre [**ayn**tray] *(between)*

The prepositions a and de merge with the masculine definite article el to form al and del respectively, e.g. Vamos al restaurante [**ba**mos al raystaoo**ran**tay] *(We are going to the restaurant)*; Vengo del hotel. [**bayn**go del o**tayl**] *(I am coming from the hotel)*.

If a personal pronoun follows a preposition, me and te become mí and ti, e.g. para mí [**pa**ra mee] *(for me)*, de ti [day tee] *(from you)*.

The preposition con merges with me and te to form conmigo [kon**mee**go] *(with me)* and contigo [kon**tee**go] *(with you)*.

Verbs

The three regular Spanish verb groups end in -ar, -er and -ir. Usually the pronoun is left out, as the subject of the verb can be identified from the verb ending.

Present tense

hablar [a**blar**] *(to speak)*:
hablo [**a**blo] *(I speak)*
hablas [**a**blas] *(you [singular/familiar] speak)*
habla [**a**bla] *(he/she speaks, you [singular/formal] speak)*
hablamos [a**bla**mos] *(we speak)*
habláis [a**blaees**] *(you [plural/familiar] speak)*
hablan [**a**blan] *(they speak, you [plural/formal] speak)*

comer [ko**mayr**] *(to eat)*:
como [**ko**mo] *(I eat)*
comes [**ko**mays] *(you [singular/familiar] eat)*
come [**ko**may] *(he/she eats, you [singular/formal] eat)*
comemos [ko**may**mos] *(we eat)*
coméis [ko**mayees**] *(you [plural/familiar] eat)*
comen [**ko**mayn] *(they eat, you [plural/formal] eat)*

abrir [abreer] *(to open):*
abro [abro] *(I open)*
abres [abrays] *(you [singular/familiar] open)*
abre [abray] *(he/she opens, you [singular/formal] open)*
abrimos [abreemos] *(we open)*
abrís [abrees] *(you [plural/familiar] open)*
abren [abrayn] *(they open, you [plural/formal] open)*

Some important irregular verbs:

tener [taynayr] *(to have):*
tengo [tayngo] *(I have)*
tienes [teeaynays] *(you [singular/familiar] have)*
tiene [teeaynay] *(he/she has, you [singular/formal] habe)*
tenemos [taynaymos] *(we have)*
tenéis [taynayees] *(you [plural/familiar] have)*
tienen [teeaynayn] *(they have, you [plural/formal] have)*

poder [podayr] *(to be able to):*
puedo [pwaydo] *(I can)*
puedes [pwaydays] *(you [singular/familiar] can)*
puede [pwayday] *(he/she can, you [singular/formal] can)*
podemos [podaymos] *(we can)*
podéis [podayees] *(you [plural/familiar] can)*
pueden [pwaydayn] *(they can, you [plural/formal] can)*

querer [kayrayr] *(to want, to wish):*
quiero [kee-ayro] *(I want)*
quieres [kee-ayrays] *(you [singular/familiar] want)*
quiere [kee-ayray] *(he/she wants, you [singular/formal] want)*
queremos [kayraymas] *(we want)*
queréis [kayrayees] *(you [plural/familiar] want)*
quieren [kee-ayrayn] *(they want, you [plural/formal] want)*

estar [aystar] *(to be)* indicating temporary or incidental properties:
estoy [aystoy] *(I am)*
estás [aystas] *(you [singular/familiar] are)*
está [aysta] *(he/she is, you [singular/formal] are)*
estamos [aystamos] *(we are)*
estáis [aystaees] *(you [plural/familiar] are)*
están [aystan] *(they are, you [plural/formal] are)*

ser [sayr] *(to be)* indicating essential, characteristic properties:
soy [soy] *(I am)*
eres [ayrays] *(you [singular/familiar] are)*
es [ays] *(he/she is, you [singular/formal] are)*
somos [somos] *(we are)*
sois [soees] *(you [plural/familiar] are)*
son [son] *(they are, you [plural/formal] are)*

Perfect tense

The perfect tense is formed with the auxiliary **haber** and the past participle of the verb. To form the past participle with regular verbs, replace the ending -ar with -ado, -er and -ir by -ido:

he [ay] *(I have)*
has [as] *(you [singular/familiar] have)*
ha [a] *(he/she has, you [singular/formal] have)*
hemos [aymos] *(we have)*
habéis [abayees] *(you [plural/familiar] have)*
han [an] *(they have, you [plural/formal] have)*

hablado [ablado] *(spoken)*
comido [komeedo] *(eaten)*
salido [saleedo] *(gone out)*

Negatives

The Spanish **no** means both no and not. The negative always goes before the verb: No hablo español [no‿ablo‿ayspan-yol] *(I don't speak Spanish.)*

Todavía no hemos comido [todabeeya no aymos komeedo] *(We haven't eaten yet.)*

Nada [nada] *(nothing)* requires a double negative: No compro nada [no kompro nada] *(I am buying nothing.)*

11

Granada, Jerez de la Frontera and Seville are important centres for Flamenco dancing. These lively festivals are occasions for women to dress up in colourful costumes

General

Hello and goodbye

Good morning/afternoon	¡Buenos días! [**bway**nos **dee**as]
Good evening	¡Buenas tardes! [**bway**nas **tar**days]
Good night	¡Buenas noches! [**bway**nas **no**chays]
Hello!	¡Hola! [**o**la]
How are you doing?	¿Qué tal? [kay tal]
How are you?	¿Cómo está/estás? [komo‿a**ysta**/ay**stas**]
Fine, thank you	Muy bien, gracias [mwee beeayn **gra**theeas]
And you?	¿Y usted/tú? [ee us**tay**/too]
Goodbye	¡Adiós! [a**deeos**]
See you soon	¡Hasta luego! [asta **looay**go]
See you tomorrow	¡Hasta mañana! [asta man-**ya**na]
Regards to the family	¡Saludos a la familia! [sa**loo**dos a la fa**meel**-eea]
Thank you for everything	Muchas gracias por todo [**moo**chas **gra**theeas por **to**do]
We really enjoyed it	Nos ha gustado mucho [nos a goo**sta**do **moo**cho]
* ¡Buen viaje! [bwen bee**akhay**]	Have a good journey!

Introducing yourself

Mr/Mrs/Miss...	Señor/Señora/Señorita [se**nyor**/se**nyora**/senyo**ree**ta]
What's your name?	¿Cómo se llama/te llamas? [**ko**mo say **ya**ma/tay **ya**mas]
My name is...	Me llamo... [may **ya**mo]
This is my husband/boyfriend.	Éste es mi marido/novio. [**ay**stay‿ays mee ma**ree**do/**no**beeo]
This is my wife/my girlfriend.	Ésta es mi esposa/novia. [**ay**stay‿ays mee ay**spo**sa/**no**beea]

12

These are my children	Éstos son mis hijos [aystos son mees eekhos]
Pleased to meet you	Encantado *(m)*/encantada *(f)* [aynkantado/aynkantada]
And you	Igualmente [eegwalmayntay]
Where are you from?	¿De dónde eres/es? [day donday_ayrays/ays]

I'm/We're	Soy/Somos [soy/somos]
from England	de Inglaterra [day_eenglatayra]
from Scotland	de Escocia [day ayscotheea]
from Wales	de Gales [day galays]
from Ireland	de Irlanda [day eerlanda]
from the USA	de los Estados Unidos [day los aystados ooneedos]
from Australia	de Australia [day aoostraleea]
from New Zealand	de Nueva Zelanda [day nooayba thaylanda]

Communication

Do you speak English?	¿Habla/Hablas inglés? [abla/ablas eenglays]
What's that called?	¿Cómo se llama eso? [komo say yama ayso]
Pardon?/Sorry?	¿Cómo? [komo]
What does that mean?	¿Qué significa eso? [kay seegneefeeka_ayso]
Did you understand that?	¿Ha/Has entendido? [a/as ayntayndeedo]
I don't understand	No entiendo [no_ayntee-ayndo]
Could you speak more slowly, please?	Más despacio, por favor [mas dayspatheeo por favor]
Could you repeat that, please?	Otro vez, por favor [otra bayth por favor]

Could you ... for me?	¿Me lo puede/puedes [may lo pwayday/pwaydays]
write that down	escribir [ayskreebeer]
explain/translate that	explicar/traducir? [ayxpleekar/tradutheer]

Civilities

Please	Por favor [por favor]
Thank you/Thank you very much	Gracias/Muchas gracias [gratheeas/moochas gratheeas]
Thank you, the same to you	Gracias, igualmente [gratheeas eegwalmayntay]
Thank you for your help	Gracias por su ayuda [gratheeas por soo_ayooda]

Greetings

Buenos días means both "good morning" and "hello" or "good-day", but from about 2pm in the afternoon and in the early evening, Spanish people will normally greet each other with "buenas tardes", and a little later on it is "buenas noches".

A more easy-going greeting, however, is a simple ¡Hola! (hello). There are two ways to say goodbye: ¡Adiós! (cheerio) or ¡Hasta luego! (see you soon!).

¿Qué tal? or ¿Cómo está? (how are you?) is often added to the initial greeting. Nobody expects an honest answer to the question. It is best to respond with bien (OK) or muy bien (very well) and then put return the question: ¿Y usted? (and you?).

13

Spanish isn't the only language you'll hear

Don't be surprised if the language you encounter in some regions of Spain is not Spanish (Castilian). In and around Barcelona and on the Balearic Islands, the main language is Catalan; in the region around Bilbao and San Sebastián the everyday language is Basque, and along the Pilgrim's Way towards Santiago de Compostela Galician is spoken. In these autonomous regions (Cata-lonia, the Basque region and Galicia) the deeply rooted regional tongues have equal status with Spanish as the official languages.

Spanish is understood and spoken throughout the whole of Spain, but not always willingly, because among the separatist communities it is still regarded as the language of dominant Castile at the heart of the central Spanish state.

You're welcome	De nada./No hay de qué [day **na**da/no‿aee de kay]
Sorry./Excuse me	Perdón. [per**don**]
It doesn't matter/Don't worry	No importa [no‿eem**por**ta]
Do you have a moment, please!	Un momento, por favor [oon mo**mayn**to por fa**vor**]
That's very nice of you	Es muy amable [ays mwee‿a**ma**blay]
I'm sorry about that	Lo siento [lo **seeayn**to]
That's a pity	¡Qué pena! [kay **pay**na]
Welcome!	¡Bienvenido! [beeaynbay**nee**do]
Congratulations!	¡Felicidades! [fayleethee**da**days]
Happy birthday!	¡Feliz cumpleaños! [fay**leeth** koomplay**an**yos]
Have fun!	¡Qué se divierta! [kay say dee**beeayr**ta]
Get well soon!	¡Qué se mejore! [kay say may**khor**ay]
Good luck!	¡Mucha suerte! [**moo**cha **swayr**tay]
Have a good journey!	¡Buen viaje! [bwen **beea**khay]
Have a good holiday!	¡Felices vacaciones! [fe**lee**thays baka**theeo**nays]
Merry Christmas!	¡Feliz Navidad! [fay**leeth** nabee**dad**]
Happy Easter!	¡Felices Pascuas! [fay**lee**thays **pas**kwas]
Happy New Year!	¡Próspero Año Nuevo! [**pros**payro‿anyo **nooay**bo]

Meeting people

Do you mind if I sit here?	¿Puedo sentarme? [**pway**do sayn**tar**may]
Do you mind?	¿Me permite? [may payr**mee**tay]
Are you	**¿Está/Estás** [ays**ta**/ays**tas**]
travelling on you own?	viajando solo *(m)*/sola *(f)*? [beea**khan**do **so**lo/**so**la]
travelling with friends?	viajando con amigos? [beea**khan**do kon a**mee**gos]
married?	casado *(m)*/casada *(f)*? [ka**sa**do/ka**sa**da]
Do you have a boyfriend/girlfriend?	¿Tienes novio/novia? [**teeay**nays **no**beeo/**no**beea]
How old are you?	¿Cuántos años tienes? [**kwan**tos **an**yos **teeay**nays]
I am 25 years old	Tengo veinticinco años [**tayn**go bayeenteetheen**ko an**yos]

What do you do for a living? ¿Cuál es su/tu profesión?
[kwal ays soo/too profe**see-yon**]
I'm still at school Voy al colegio [boy al ko**lay**kheeo]
I'm a student Soy estudiante [soy‿aystoo**deean**tay]
I'm employed Soy empleado *(m)*/empleada *(f)*
[soy‿aymplayado/aymplayada]
Can I buy you a drink? ¿Quiere tomar algo? [**keeay**ray to**mar al**go]
Thank you, that would be Sí, con mucho gusto [see kon **moo**cho **goos**to]
nice
Good idea Buena idea [**bway**na‿ee**da**ya]
Why not? ¿Por qué no? [por kay no]
No, thank you No, gracias [no **gra**theeas]
Perhaps another time Tal vez otro día [tal **bayth o**tro **dee**a]
Maybe later Tal vez más tarde [tal **bayth** mas **tar**day]
Do you like it here? ¿Le/Te gusta aquí? [lay/tay **goos**ta‿a**kee**]
I like it very much here Me gusta mucho [may **goos**ta **moo**cho]
Is this your first time here? ¿Es la primera vez que está/estás aquí?
[ays la pree**may**ra bayth kay‿ay**sta**/ay**stas** a**kee**]
No, I've been to... before. No, ya he estado en... [no ya‿ay‿ay**sta**do‿ayn]
Have you ever been to ¿Conoce/Conoces Inglaterra?
England? [kono**thay**/kono**thays** eengla**tay**ra]
You have to visit me Tiene/Tienes que visitarme un día
[**teeay**nay/**teeay**nays kay veesee**tar**may‿un
deea]

Here's my address Ésta es mi dirección [**ays**ta‿ays mee
deerayk**thee**on]
How long have you been ¿Cuánto tiempo lleva/llevas aquí?
staying here? [**kwan**to **teeaym**po **yay**-va/**yay**-vas a**kee**]
For a week./For two days Una semana/Dos días [**oo**na say**ma**na/
dos **dee**as]
How much longer are you ¿Cuánto tiempo se queda/te quedas aquí?
staying? [**kwan**to **teeaym**po say **kay**da/tay **kay**das
a**kee**]
Another week/two days Una semana/Dos días más
[**oo**na say**ma**na/dos **dee**as mas]

Shall we ... together today/ **¿Hoy/Mañana vamos juntos?**
tomorrow? [oy/man**ya**na **ba**mos **khun**tos]
have a meal a comer [a ko**mayr**]
go to the cinema/go al cine/a bailar [al **thee**nay/a **baee**lar]
dancing
do something sporty a hacer deporte [a‿a**thayr** day**por**tay]
play a jugar? [a khoo**gar**]
Shall we go out together ¿Vamos a salir juntos hoy/mañana?
today/tomorrow? [**ba**mos a sa**leer khun**tos oy/man-**ya**na]
O.K.! Muy bien/Vale [**mwee** bee**ayn**/**ba**lay]
No, I don't want to No, no tengo ganas [no no **tayn**go **ga**nas]
I can't, sorry Lo siento, pero no puedo
[lo **seeayn**to **pay**ro no **pway**do]
What time/Where shall we ¿Cuándo/Dónde nos encontramos?
meet? [**kwan**do/**don**day nos aynkon**tra**mos]
At 9 o'clock in front of the A las nueve delante del cine
cinema [a las **nooay**bay day**lan**tay dayl **thee**nay]

15

Shall I	**¿Puedo [pway**do]
pick you up	llevarle/llevarte [yay**var**lay/yay**var**tay]
take you home	acompañarle/-te a casa
	[akompan**yar**lay/-tay a ka**sa**]
take you to the bus stop?	acompañarle/-te al autobús?
	[akompan**yar**lay/-tay al aooto**boos**]
No, that's not necessary	No, no es necesario. [no no ays naythay**sa**reeo]
It's been a wonderful	Ha sido un día maravilloso/una noche
day/evening	maravillosa [a seedo oon deea marabee**yo**so/
	oona nochay marabee**yo**sa]
When can we see each other	¿Cuándo vamos a encontrarnos?
again?	[**kwan**do bamos a aynkon**trar**nos]
I don't like that	Eso no me gusta [**ay**so no may **goo**sta]
I don't feel like it	No tengo ganas [no **tayn**go **ga**nas]
Leave me alone!	¡Déjeme/Déjame en paz!
	[**day**khaymay/**day**khamay ayn path]
Please go away!	¡Por favor váyase/vete! [por fa**vor bay**asay/
	baytay]

Questions

What's that?	¿Qué es esto? [kay ays **ay**sto]
How much is that?	¿Cuánto cuesta? [**kwan**to **kway**sta]
Where is...?/can I get...?	¿Dónde está/hay...? [**don**day ay**sta**/aee]
Where does... go?	¿Adónde va...? [a**don**day ba]
What's that called?	¿Cómo se llama esto? [**ko**mo say yama ay**sto**]
How long does it last?	¿Cuánto tiempo dura? [**kwan**to teeaympo
	doora]
When does the concert start?	¿Cuándo empieza el concierto?
	[**kwan**do aympeeaytha ayl kontheeayrto]
How many kilometres/	¿Cuántos kilómetros/minutos son?
minutes is it?	[**kwan**tos keelomaytros/mee**noo**tos son]
Could you	**¿Puede usted [pway**day **oo**stay]
help me	ayudarme [ayoo**dar**may]
show me, please?	mostrarmelo? [mos**trar**maylo]
Can I help you?	¿Puedo ayudarle? [**pway**do ayoo**dar**lay]

Interrogatives

What?	¿Qué? [kay]
Who?	¿Quién? [keeayn]
Which?	¿Cuál? *(Sing)*/¿Cuáles? *(Pl)* [kwal/**kwa**lays]
Where?	¿Dónde? [**don**day]
Where to?	¿Adónde? [a**don**day]
How?	¿Cómo? [**ko**mo]
How much/how many?	¿Cuánto(s)? [**kwan**to(s)]
When?	¿Cuándo? [**kwan**do]
How long?	¿Cuánto tiempo? [**kwan**to teeaympo]
Why?	¿Por qué? [por kay]
What for?	¿Para qué? [para kay]

Time

What's the (exact) time, please?	¿Por favor, qué hora es (exactamente)? [por fa**vor** kay‿ora‿ays (ayxakta**mayn**tay)]

It's
- one o'clock
- noon/midnight

Es [es]
- la una [la‿**oo**na]
- mediodía/medianoche [maydeeo**dee**a/maydeea**no**chay]

It's
- 2 o'clock/3 o'clock
- quarter past three
- quarter to five

- twenty past three
- half past three
- five to six

Son [son]
- las dos/las tres [las dos/las trays]
- las tres y cuarto [las trays ee **kwar**to]
- las cinco menos cuarto [las **theen**ko **may**nos **kwar**to]
- las tres y veinte [las trays ee **bay-een**tay]
- las tres y media [las trays ee **may**deea]
- las seis menos cinco [las say-ees **may**nos **theen**ko]

What time do we have to be there?
¿A qué hora tenemos que estar allí? [a kay‿ora tay**nay**mos kay‿ay**star** a-**yee**]

* A eso de las doce [a‿**e**so de las **do**thay]
Around twelve

* A las trece en punto [a las **tray**thay‿en **poon**to]
At one o'clock sharp

When is breakfast/ lunch/dinner?
¿A qué hora es el desayuno/la comida/la cena? [a kay‿ora **ays**‿ayl daysa-**yoo**no/la ko**mee**da/**thay**na]

* De ocho a nueve [day‿**o**cho‿a **nooay**bay]
From eight to nine

* Entre las siete y las ocho [**ayn**tray las **seeay**tay‿ee las **o**cho]
Between seven and eight

* Dentro de una hora [**dayn**tro day‿**oo**na‿**o**ra]
In one hour

17

Date

What's the date today?	¿A cuántos estamos? [a **kwan**tos ays**ta**mos]
Today's the 1st/2nd/15th of August	Hoy es el uno/dos/quince de agosto [oy‿ays ayl **oo**no/dos/**keen**thay day‿a**gos**to]
We'll arrive on the 20th of May	Llegamos el veinte de mayo [yay**ga**mos ayl bay-**een**tay day **ma**eeo]
We're staying until August 31st	Nos quedamos hasta el treinta y uno de agosto [nos kay**da**mos **as**ta‿ayl tray-**een**ta‿ee‿**oo**no day‿a**gos**to]
I was born/my birthday is on December 19th (1964)	**Nací/Mi cumpleaños es** [na**thee**/mee coompla**ya**nyos ays] el diecinueve de diciembre (de mil novecientos sesentacuatro) [ayl deeaythee**noo**aybay day‿deethee-**aym**bray (day meel nobay**thee**ayntos say**sayn**takwatro)]

Indication of time

in the evening	por la noche [por la **no**chay]
at the weekend	el fin de semana [el feen day say**ma**na]
until tomorrow	¡hasta mañana! [**as**ta man**ya**na]
early (in the morning)	temprano (por la mañana) [taym**pra**no (por la man**ya**na)]
yesterday	ayer [a-**yayr**]
today	hoy [oy]
tonight	hoy por la noche [oy por la **no**chay]
in a fortnight	dentro de quince días [**dayn**tro day **keen**thay **dee**as]

Days of the week

Monday lunes [**loo**nays]
Tuesday martes [**mar**tays]
Wednesday miércoles [meea**yr**kolays]
Thursday jueves [khoo**ay**bays]
Friday viernes [beea**yr**nays]
Saturday sábado [**sa**bado]
Sunday domingo [do**meen**go]

Months

January enero [ay**nay**ro]
February febrero [fay**bray**ro]
March marzo [**mar**tho]
April abril [a**breel**]
May mayo [**ma**eeyo]
June junio [**khoo**neeo]

July julio [**khoo**leeo]
August agosto [a**gos**to]
September septiembre [sep**teea**ymbray]
October octubre [oc**too**bray]
November noviembre [no**beea**ymbray]
December diciembre [deethee**ay**mbray]

Seasons

spring primavera [preema**bay**ra]
summer verano [be**ra**no]
autumn otoño [o**to**nyo]
winter invierno [een**beea**yrno]

peak/off peak season temporada alta/baja [tempo**ra**da‿**al**ta/**ba**kha]

(this/next/last/every) year	(este/el próximo/el pasado/cada) año [(**ays**tay/ayl **pro**xeemo/ayl pasado/**ka**da) anyo]
now	ahora [a-**o**ra]
sometimes	a veces [a **bay**thays]
minute	minuto [mee**noo**to]
at midday	a mediodía [a maydeeo**dee**a]
tomorrow	mañana [man**yan**a]
in the morning	mañana por la mañana [man**yan**a por la man**yan**a]
in the afternoon	por la tarde [por la **tar**day]
at night	por la noche [por la **no**chay]
in time	a tiempo [a **teeaym**po]
second	segundo [se**goon**do]
late/too late	tarde/demasiado tarde [**tar**day/daymaseeado **tar**day]
later	más tarde [mas **tar**day]
hour	hora [**o**ra]
daily	cada día [**ka**da **dee**a]
day	día [**dee**a]
day after tomorrow	pasado mañana [pa**sa**do man**yan**a]
(two days) ago	hace (dos días) [**a**thay (dos **dee**as)]
day before yesterday	anteayer [antay-a**yer**]
before	antes [**an**tays]
in the morning	por la mañana [por la man**yan**a]
week	semana [say**ma**na]
at the moment	actualmente [actooal**mayn**tay]

Measurements

centimetre/metre/kilometre	centímetro/metro/kilómetro [thayn**tee**maytro/**may**tro/keelo**may**tro]
square metre/square kilometre/hectare	metro cuadrado/kilómetro cuadrado/hectárea [**may**tro kwa**dra**do/keelo**may**tro kwa**dra**do/ek**tah**raya]
cubic metre	metro cúbico [**may**tro **koo**beeko]
kilometres per hour	kilómetro por hora [keelo**may**tro por **o**ra]
quarter of a litre	un cuarto litro [oon **kwar**to **lee**tro]
half a litre	medio litro [**may**deeo **lee**tro]
gram/half a kilo/ kilogram/ton	gramo/medio kilo/kilo/tonelada [**gra**mo/**may**deeo **kee**lo/**kee**lo/tonay**la**da]
second/minute/hour	segundo/minuto/hora [say**goon**do/mee**noo**to/**o**ra]
day/week/month/year	día/semana/mes/año [**dee**a/say**ma**na/mays/anyo]
a dozen	docena [do**thay**na]
a couple	par [par]
a portion	ración [rathee**on**]

Weather

What a beautiful day!	¡Qué buen tiempo hace hoy! [kay bwayn **teeaym**po⌣**a**thay⌣oy]
Is it going to stay nice/ horrible?	¿Seguirá el buen/mal tiempo? [se**gee**ra el bwen/mal **teeaym**po]
What does the weather report say?	¿Qué dicen en la previsión del tiempo? [kay **dee**thayn ayn la prayvee**see**on dayl **teeaym**po]
It's going to get colder/warmer	¿Las temperaturas bajarán/subirán? [las taympayra**too**ras bakha**ran**/soobee**ran**]
It is hot/close/windy	Hace mucho calor/bochorno/viento [**a**thay **moo**cho ka**lor**/bo**chor**no/**beeayn**to]
It is stormy/foggy	Hay tempestad/niebla [aee taympay**sta**/**neeay**bla]
It is going to rain/snow today/tomorrow	¿Hoy/Mañana lloverá/nevará? [oy/ma**nya**na yo**bay**ra/ne**ba**ra]
For how long has it been raining?	¿Llueve desde hace mucho tiempo? [**yooay**bay **days**day⌣**a**thay **moo**cho **teeaym**po]
When is it going to stop raining?	¿Cuándo terminará la lluvia? [**kwan**do taymee**na**ra la **yoo**beea]
What's the temperature?	¿Cuántos grados hay? [**kwan**tos **gra**dos aee]
25 degrees (in the shade)	Veinticinco grados (a la sombra) [be-eentee**theen**ko **gra**dos (a la **som**bra)]

Colours

I'm looking for a pair of black trousers	Estoy buscando unos pantalones negros [ay**stoy** boo**skan**do **oo**nos panta**lo**nays **nay**gros]
Do you have this shirt?	**¿Tiene esta camisa?** [tee**ay**nay⌣**ay**sta ka**mee**sa]
in white, too?	también en blanco? [tam**beeayn** ayn **blan**ko]
in another colour?	en otro color? [ayn **o**tro ko**lor**]
I don't like this colour	Este color no me gusta [**ay**stay ko**lor** no may **goo**sta]
This colour is too light/dark	Este color es demasiado claro/oscuro [**ay**stay ko**lor** ays dayma**see**ado **kla**ro/o**skoo**ro]

Colours and patterns

black negro [**nay**gro]	**orange** naranja [na**rankh**a]
blonde rubio [**roo**beeo]	**patterned** con dibujo [kon dee**book**ho]
blue azul [a**thool**]	**pink** rosa [**ro**sa]
brown marrón [ma**ron**]	**plain-coloured** liso [**lee**so]
checked a cuadros [a **kwa**dros]	**purple** purpúreo [poor**poo**rayo]
beige beige [bay-**eesch**]	**red** rojo [**rokh**o]
dark oscuro [o**skoo**ro]	**striped** rayado [ra-**ya**do]
green verde [**bayr**day]	**white** blanco [**blan**ko]
grey gris [grees]	**yellow** amarillo [ama**ree**lyo]
light claro [**kla**ro]	

The highest permissible speed on the autovías (inter-city highways) is 100kmph (62mph), on the autopistas (motorways) it is 120kmph (74mph)

Getting Around

Customs formalities

* ¡Su pasaporte! [soo pasa**por**tay]
Your passport, please!

* ¡Su carnet de conducir! [soo kar**nay** day kondoo**theer**]
Your driving licence, please!

* ¡Los documentos del coche! [los dokoo**mayn**tos del **ko**chay]
Your registration papers, please!

* ¡Los pasaportes de los hijos! [los pasa**por**tays day los **ee**khos]
The children's passports, please!

* ¡La carta verde, por favor! [la **kar**ta **bayr**day por fa**vor**]
Your green insurance card, please!

* ¿Adónde va? [a**don**day ba]
Where are you going to?

I'm/We're going to...
Voy/Vamos a... (**bo**ee/**ba**mos a]

I am a tourist
Soy turista [soee too**ree**sta]

I am on a business trip
Hago un viaje de negocios [**a**go oon **bee**akhay day ne**go**theeos]

* ¿Tiene algo que declarar? [tee**ay**nay␣**al**go kay daykla**rar**]
Do you have anything to declare?

No, I have nothing to declare
No, no tengo nada que declarar [no no **tayn**go **na**da kay daykla**rar**]

I have just a few presents
Sólo algunos regalos [**so**lo al**goo**nos ray**ga**los]

Do I have to pay duty on this?
¿Tengo que declarar esto? [**tayn**go kay dayklarar **ays**to]

* Está prohibido llevar eso [ay**sta** proee**bee**do yay-**var** **ay**so]
You aren't allowed to import this!

* ¡Abra por favor la maleta! [**abra** por fa**vor** la ma**lay**ta]
Open the suitcase, please!

21

How many... are duty free?	¿Cuántos... están exentos de aduana?
	[kwantos... aystan ayxayntos day⌣adooana]
cigarettes	cigarrillos [theegareeyos]
litres of wine	litros de vino [leetros day beeno]

Asking directions

How do I get	¿Cómo voy [komo boee]
to ...	a ... [a]
onto the motorway	a la autopista [a la⌣aootopeesta]
to the city centre	al centro [al thayntro]
to ... Square	a la plaza de ... [a la platha day]
to ... Street	a la calle de ... [a la kayay day]
to the station (bus station)/	a la estación (de autobuses)/al aeropuerto [a
to the airport	la estatheeon (day aootobooses)/al
to the harbour?	aeeropwayrto]/al puerto? [al pwayrto]
* En el cruce [ayn ayl kroothay]	At the crossroads
* En el semáforo	At the traffic lights
[ayn ayl saymaforo]	

* Después de quinientos	After 500 metres
metros [despooays day	
keeneeayntos maytros]	
* girar a la derecha/a la	turn right/left
izquierda [kheerar a la	
dayraycha/a la⌣eethkeeayrda]	
* ir todo recto [eer todo rekto]	go straight ahead
* volver atrás [bolbayr atras]	turn around
Is this the road to...?	¿Es la carretera a...? [ays la karaytayra⌣a]
How many metres/kilometres	¿Cuántos metros/kilómetros son a...?
is it to...?	[kwantos maytros/keelomaytros son a]
Can you show me that on the	¿Puede mostrármelo en el mapa?
map?	[pwayday mostrarmaylo⌣ayn ayl mapa]

Car, motorbike and bicycle hire

I'd like to hire	Quería alquilar [kayreea⌣alkeelar]
a car	un coche [oon kochay]
a four wheel drive	un coche todo terreno
	[oon kochay todo tayrrayno]
a minibus	un microbús [oon meekroboos]
a camper van	un coche-vivienda [oon kochay beebeeaynda]
a motorbike	una moto [oona moto]
a moped/a motorised	un ciclomotor/velomotor
bicycle	[oon theeklomotor/baylomotor]
a scooter	un motoscooter [oon motoskootayr]
a bicycle/a mountainbike	una bicicleta/bicicleta de montaña
	[oona beetheeklayta/beetheeklayta day
	montanya]
for two days/one week	para dos días/una semana
	[para dos deeas/oona saymana]
from today/tomorrow	a partir de hoy/mañana.
	[a parteer day⌣oy/man-yana]

What do you charge	¿Cuánto cuesta el vehículo
	[kwanto kwaysta‿el bayeekoolo]
per day/per week	por día/por semana [por **dee**a/por say**ma**na]
per kilometre?	por kilómetro? [por kee**lo**maytro]
Is there a charge per kilometre?	¿Hay un kilómetraje limitado? [aee‿oon keelomay**tra**khay leemee**ta**do]
How many kilometres are included in the price?	¿Cuántos kilómetros están incluídos en el precio? [**kwan**tos keelomaytros ays**tan** eenkloo**ee**dos ayn ayl **pray**theeo]
How much petrol is left in the tank?	¿Cuántos litros de gasolina hay en el depósito? [**kwan**tos **lee**tros day gaso**lee**na aee ayn ayl day**po**seeto]
What petrol does it take?	¿Qué gasolina tengo que poner? [kay gaso**lee**na **tayn**go kay po**nayr**]
How much is the deposit?	¿Cuánto es la caución? [**kwan**to ays la kaoo**theeon**]
Does the vehicle have comprehensive insurance?	¿El vehículo está asegurado a todo riesgo? [ayl bayeekoolo‿ays**ta**‿asaygoo**ra**do a **to**do **reeay**sgo]
How high is the excess?	¿Qué parte de los daños tengo que asumir yo? [kay **par**tay day los **dan**-yos **tayn**go kay‿asoo**meer** yo]
Can I take the car back in...?	¿Puedo devolver el vehículo en...? [**pway**do daybol**bayr** ayl bayeekoolo‿ayn]
When do I have to be back by?	¿Hasta cuándo tengo que devolver el vehículo? [asta **kwan**dò **tayn**go kay daybol**bayr** ayl bayeekoolo]

Traffic signs

Atasco traffic jam
Atención caution
Autopista (de peaje) motorway (subject to toll)
Callejón sin salida cul-de-sac
Carril-bici cycle track
Ceda el paso give way
Circunvalación bypass
Conducir por la derecha keep right
Control de radar radar control
Curva peligrosa dangerous bend
Desviación/Desvío detour
Dirección única one-way street
Escuela school
Aparcamiento/Estacionamiento/Parking car park
Giro obligatorio roundabout
Hospital hospital
Obras road works
Paso a nivel (sin barrera) (ungated) level crossing
Paso de cebra zebra crossing
Paso de peatones pedestrian crossing
Peaje toll booth
Peligro danger
Precaución caution
Prohibido adelantar no overtaking
Prohibido el paso no thoroughfare
Prohibido estacionar no parking
Prohibido girar a la izquierda no left turn
Prohibido parar no stopping
Respetar la preferencia give way
Salida exit
Sentido único one-way street
Todas direcciones all directions
Zona azul short-term car park
Zona de peatones pedestrian precinct
Obras de carretera road works
Puente bajo low bridge

23

Travelling by car

Spanish motorists are able to use the many motorway-style roads (autovías) free of charge, but some motorways are toll roads (autopistas). At the tollbooths (peajes) for short stretches of motorway, e.g. by-pass sections, there are usually rapid payment facilities.

If you have the right amount of change to hand, you can insert the sum indicated into the machine, so always keep some loose coins handy.

Do not risk parking in unauthorised places. The tow-away teams (la grúa) are always quick off the mark. The other possibility is a wheel-clamp (el cepo). To park in town centres, you must purchase a parking ticket from the machine. Most Spanish petrol stations are manned and you pay the attendant, who also appreciates a small tip for performing extra services, e.g. cleaning windscreen, checking tyres.

Could you explain how everything works, please!	¡Explíqueme todas las funciones, por favor! [ayx**plee**kamay **to**das las foonk**theeo**nays por fa**vor**]

Parking

Can I park here?	¿Puedo aparcar el coche aquí? [**pway**do‿apar**kar** ayl **ko**chay‿a**kee**]
Is there a... near here?	¿**Hay por aquí** [aee por‿a**kee**]
a (supervised) car park	un aparcamiento (vigilado) [oon aparka**meeayn**to (beekhee**la**do)]
a car park/garage?	un garaje? [oon ga**ra**khay]
Is the car park open during the night?	¿El garaje está abierto por la noche? [ayl ga**ra**khay‿esta‿a**beeayr**to por la **no**chay]
* Ocupado [okoo**pa**do]	Full
How much is it	¿**Cuánto cuesta** [**kwan**to **kway**sta]
per hour	por hora [por **oh**ra]
per day	por día [por **dee**a]
per night?	por noche? [por **no**chay]

Petrol

Where's the nearest petrol station, please?	¿Dónde hay una gasolinera por aquí? [**don**day‿aee‿**oo**na gasolee**nay**ra por‿a**kee**]
Fill up, please./20 litres of ... please	¡Lleno, por favor/veinte litros [**yay**no por fa**vor**/**bayeen**tay **lee**tros]
regular	de gasolina normal [day gaso**lee**na nor**mal**]
super	de súper [day **soo**payr]
diesel	de diesel/de gasóleo [day **dee**sayl/day ga**so**layo]
unleaded/leaded.	sin plomo/con plomo [seen **plo**mo/kon **plo**mo]
I'd like half a litre of oil, please	Quería medio litro de aceite [kay**ree**a **may**deeo **lee**tro day‿a**thay**eetay]
Please check	¡**Compruebe por favor** [kom**prooay**bay por fa**vor**]
the oil	el nivel del aceite [ayl nee**bayl** day‿a**thay**eetay]
the water	el agua del radiador [ayl **a**gooa dayl radeea**dor**]

Breakdown and accident

I have a flat tyre

Tengo una rueda pinchada
[**tayn**go **oo**na **roo**ayda peen**cha**da]

My car's broken down

Tengo una avería [**tayn**go oona‿avay**ree**a]

I've had an accident

Tengo un accidente [**tayn**go oon akthee**dayn**tay]

Could you give me a lift

¿Podría usted llevarme [po**dree**a‿oo**stay** yay-**var**may]

to the nearest petrol station

a una gasolinera [a‿**oo**na gasolee**nay**ra]

to a garage?

a un taller? [a‿oon ta-**yayr**]

Could you

¿Podría usted [po**dree**a oo**stay**]

tow my car away

remolcarme [raymol**kar**may]

help me

ayudarme [aeeoo**dar**may]

help me jump-start my car

ayudarme a arrancar [aeeoo**dar**may‿a‿a**rran**kar]

lend me your jack

prestarme su gato [pray**star**may soo **ga**to]

call the police/fire brigade

llamar a la policía/a los bomberos
[ya**mar** a la polee**thee**a/a los bom**bay**ros]

call an ambulance

llamar a la ambulancia
[ya**mar** a la amboo**lan**theea]

call a doctor?

llamar a un médico? [ya**mar** a oon **may**deeko]

Are you injured?

¿Está usted herido *(m)*/herida *(f)*?
[ay**sta**‿oo**stay**‿ay**ree**do/ay**ree**da]

Nobody is injured

No hay heridos [no‿aee‿ay**ree**dos]

Somebody is (seriously) injured

Hay una persona herida (gravemente)
[aee‿**oo**na payr**so**na‿ay**ree**da (gravay**mayn**tay)]

Give me..., please.

¡Por favor, deme [por fa**vor day**may]

your name and address

su nombre y su dirección
[soo **nom**bray‿ee soo deerayk**thee**on]

the name and address of your insurance company

nombre y dirección de su compañía de seguros! [**nom**bray‿ee deerayk**thee**on day soo kompa**nee**a day say**goo**ros]

The magnificent centre of Seville's old city viewed from the Santa María cathedral

25

Car, motorbike, bicycle

automatic gear box	cambio automático [**kam**beeo⏜aooto**ma**teeko]
battery	batería [batay**ree**a]
bicycle tyre	cubierta [koo**beeayr**ta]
break	freno [**frayno**]
car key	llave del coche *(f)* [**ya**-vay dayl **ko**chay]
catalytic converter	catalizador *(m)* [kataleetha**dor**]
child seat	asiento de niños [a**seeayn**to day **neen**-yos]
clutch	embrague *(m)* [aym**bra**gay]
engine	motor *(m)* [mo**tor**]
exhaust	escape *(m)* [ays**ka**pay]
fan belt	correa trapezoidal [ko**ray**a trapaythoee**dal**]
first-aid kit	botiquín *(m)* [botee**keen**]
fuse	fusible *(m)* [foo**see**blay]
gearshift	cambio de marchas [**kam**beeo day **mar**chas]
hand-brake	freno de mano [**frayno** day **mano**]
headlights	faro [**faro**]
helmet	casco [**kas**ko]
horn	bocina [bo**thee**na]
light bulb	bombilla [bom**bee**ya]
puncture repair kit	estuche de reparación *(m)* [**estoo**chay day repara**theeon**]
pump	bomba de inflar/bomba neumática [**bom**ba day⏜een**flar**/**bom**ba nayoo**ma**teeka]
rear light	luz trasera *(f)* [looth tra**sayr**a]
repair	reparación *(f)* [raypara**theeon**]
screw	tornillo [tor**nee**yo]
screwdriver	destornillador *(m)* [daystornee-ya**dor**]
seat belt	cinturón de seguridad *(m)* [theentoo**ron** day saygoo**ree**dad]
short circuit	cortocircuito [kortotheerkoo**ee**to]
spare part	pieza de recambio [**peeay**tha day ray**kam**beeo]
spare tyre	rueda de reserva [**rooay**da day ray**sayr**va]
spark plugs	bujía [bu**khee**a]
steering	dirección *(f)* [deerayk**theeon**]
tank	depósito [day**po**seeto]
tow rope	cable de remolque *(m)* [**kab**lay day raymol**kay**]
tools	herramientas *(f/pl)* [eramee**ayn**tas]
tyre	neumático [nayoo**ma**teeko]
tube	cámara de aire [**ka**mara day⏜a**eer**ay]
valve	válvula [**val**voola]
warning triangle	triángulo de peligro [tree**an**goolo day pay**lee**gro]
windscreen wipers	limpiaparabrisas *(m)* [leempeeapara**bree**sas]

I was/You were/He was	He ido/Usted ha ido/Ha ido [aee‿eedo/oostay‿a‿eedo/a‿eedo]
driving too fast	demasiado rápido [daymaseeado rapeedo]
driving too close	con muy poca distancia [kon mooee poka deestantheea]
I/You/He	No he/Usted no ha/No ha [no‿aee/oostay no‿a/no‿a]
ignored the right of way	respetado la preferencia [rayspaytado la prayfayrayntheea]
went through a red light	respetado la luz roja [rayspaytado la looth rokha]
Did you witness the accident?	¿Es usted testigo del accidente? [es oostay taysteego dayl aktheedayntay]
Thank you very much for your help	Muchas gracias por su ayuda [moochas gratheeas por soo ayooda]

Garage

Where's the nearest Seat garage?	¿Hay por aquí un concesionario Seat? [aee por‿akee oon konthayseeonareeo sayat]
The engine	El motor [el motor]
won't start	no arranca [no‿aranka]
is losing oil	pierde aceite [peeayrday‿athayeetay]
isn't working	no marcha bien [no marcha beeayn]
The brakes don't work	Los frenos no funcionan bien [los fraynos no foonktheeonan beeayn]
The warning light is on	La lámpara piloto está encendida [la lampara peeloto esta‿aynthayndeeda]
The exhaust is faulty	El escape está estropeado [el ayskapay‿esta aystropayado]
The radiator is leaking	El radiador está permeable [el radeeador esta payrmayablay]
How much will the repairs be?	¿Cuánto cuesta la reparación? [kwanto kwaysta la rayparatheeon]
When will the car be ready?	¿Cuándo estará listo? [kwando‿estara leesto]

Hitchhiking

Are you going to...?	¿Usted va a...? [oostay ba‿a]
Could you give me a lift to...?	¿Puede llevarme a...? [pwayday yayvarmay‿a]
I'd like to get out here, please!	Quiero bajar aquí [keeayro bakhar akee]
Thanks, and have a good trip!	Gracias y ¡buen viaje! [gratheeas ee bwen beeakhay]

Public transport

Bus, tram and underground

Is there a bus to...?	¿Hay un autobús a...? [aee‿oon aootoboos a]
How long does it take?	¿Cuánto tiempo dura el viaje? [kwanto teeaympo doora‿el beeakhay]

Excuse me, where's the nearest
  bus stop
  tram stop
  underground station?
Is it far?
Which tube line goes to...?

When does the last bus leave?
Which line must I take?

How many stops is it?

Does this tube go to...?

Where do I have to
  get off/change
  get to the station
  get to the city centre?
Could you tell me when I have to get off, please.
Where can I buy a ticket?

A ticket to..., please

How much is it?

Could you stop here, please!

Taxi

Where's the nearest taxi rank?
  To the station!
To the hotel!
To the airport!
To the centre of town!
To..., please!
How much is it to...?

Could you switch on the meter, please?
Could you wait/stop here, please.
That's for you!

¿Dónde está la próxima
[donday⌣esta la proxeema]
  parada del autobús [parada dayl aootoboos]
  parada del tranvía [parada dayl tranbeea]
  estación del metro? [estatheeon dayl maytro]
¿Está lejos? [esta laykhos]
¿Cuál es el metro para...?
[kwal ays ayl maytro para]
¿A qué hora regresa el último autobús?
[a kay⌣ora raygraysa⌣ayl oolteemo aootoboos]
¿Qué dirección tengo que tomar?
[kay deerayktheeon tayngo kay tomar]
¿Cuántas paradas son?
[kwantas paradas son]
¿Es el metro para...?
[es el maytro para]

¿Dónde tengo que [donday tayngo kay]
  bajar/cambiar [bakhar/kambeear]
  para la estación [para la⌣aystatheeon]
  para el centro? [para⌣ayl thayntro]
¡Dígame por favor, cuando tengo que bajar!
[deegamay por favor kwando tayngo kay bakhar]
¿Dónde puedo comprar ayl billete?
[donday pwaydo komprar ayl bee-yaytay]
Un billete a... por favor
[oon bee-yaytay a... por favor]
¿Cuánto cuesta el billete?
[kwanto kwaysta⌣ayl bee-yaytay]
¡Pare aquí, por favor! [paray akee por favor]

¿Dónde hay una parada de taxis por aquí?
[donday⌣aee⌣oona parada day taxees por⌣akee]
¡A la estación! [a la⌣aystatheeon]
¡Al hotel! [al⌣otayl]
¡Al aeropuerto! [al ayropwayrto]
¡Al centro! [al thayntro]
¡A..., por favor! [a... por favor]
¿Cuál es el precio hasta/al/a la...?
[kwal es el praytheeo asta/al/a la]
¡Ponga el taxímetro por favor!
[ponga el taxeemaytro por favor]
¡Espere/Pare aquí por favor!
[ayspayray/paray⌣akee por favor]
¡Para usted! [para⌣oostay]

Getting around by train and bus

Where's the (bus) station, please?

¿Dónde está la estación (de autobuses), por favor? [donday⌣aysta la aystatheeon (de aootobooses) por favor]

When's the next train/ bus to ...?	¿Cuándo sale el tren/autobús a...? [kwando salay⌣el trayn/aootoboos a]
Do I have to change?	¿Tengo que hacer trasbordo? [tayngo kay⌣athayr trasbordo]
Which platform does the train leave from?	¿De qué andén sale el tren? [day kay andayn salay⌣el trayn]
When does the train/bus arrive in...?	¿Cuándo llega el tren/autobús a...? [kwando yay-ga⌣el trayn/aootoboos a]
Is there a connection to... in...?	¿En... tengo enlace para...? [ayn... tayngo⌣enlathay para]
How much is it?	¿Cuánto cuesta el billete? [kwanto kwaysta⌣el bee-yaytay]
Are there special rates for	¿Hay un descuento para [aee⌣oon dayskwaynto para]
children	niños [neenyos]
senior citizen?	la tercera edad? [la tayrthayra⌣ayda]

One ticket/... tickets, please ¡Por favor un billete/unos billetes [por favor oon bee-yaytay/oonos bee-yaytays]

to...	a... [a]
single/return	de ida/de ida y vuelta [day⌣eeda/day⌣eeda⌣ee vooaylta]
first-class/second-class	de primera/segunda clase [day preemayra/saygoonda klasay]
for two adults and two children!	para dos adultos y dos niños [para dos adooltos ee dos neenyos]

I'd like to book ... Quería reservar [kayreea raysayrvar]

a (window) seat	un asiento (junto a la ventanilla) [oon aseeaynto (khoonto⌣a la vayntaneeya)]
a (non-) smoker seat	(no) fumadores [(no) foomadorays]
a couchette	un billete de coche-literas [oon bee-yaytay day kochay leetayras]

Signs

¡Agua no potable! no drinking water	Información information
Andén platform	Lavabo washroom
Coche-cama sleeper/sleeping car	Lavabos toilets
Coche-literas couchette	libre vacant
Coche-restaurante dining car	ocupado occupied
Freno de alarma emergency brake	Salida exit/departure
	Vía platform

a sleeper

un billete de coche-cama
[oon bee-**yay**tay day **ko**chay **ka**ma]

on the two o'clock
train/bus

para el tren/autobús a las catorce horas
[**para**ˍayl trayn/aooto**boos** a las
ka**tor**thayˍ**o**hras]

I'd like
to take my bicycle with me.
to check in my luggage.

Quería [kay**ree**a]
llevar la bicicleta [yay**var** la beethee**klay**ta]
facturar el equipaje [faktoo**rar** ayl
aykee**pa**khay]

Where can I find... , please?
the left-luggage office
the lockers

Por favor, ¿dónde está [por favor don**day**ˍa**ysta**]
la consigna [la kon**seeg**na]
la consigna automática?
[la kon**seeg**naˍaooto**ma**teeka]

Is this the train/bus to...?

¿Éste es el tren/autobús para...?
[**ays**tay ays ayl trayn/aooto**boos** **pa**ra]

Is this seat taken, please?

¿Este asiento está libre?
[**ays**tay a**seeayn**toˍa**ysta** **lee**bray]

Getting around by plane

I'd like to
to book a flight to...

Quería [kay**ree**a]
reservar un vuelo a... [raysayr**var** oon
vwaylo**ˍ**a]

for 1 person
for two/four persons

para una persona [**para**ˍ**oo**na pay**rso**na]
para dos/cuatro personas
[**pa**ra dos/**kwa**tro pay**rso**nas]

on 2nd September

el dos de septiembre [ayl dos day
sep**teeaym**bray]

one-way/return

de ida/de ida y vuelta
[dayˍ**ee**da/dayˍ**ee**daˍee **vooayl**ta]

economy class/first class.

de clase turista/de primera clase
[day **kla**say too**ree**sta/day pree**may**ra **kla**say]

to confirm a return flight
to cancel the flight/change
the flight

confirmar el vuelo [konfeer**mar** el **vway**lo]
anular/cambiar el vuelo
[anoo**lar**/kam**bee**ar el **vway**lo]

Are there any... seats left?

¿Hay todavía plazas libres
[aee toda**bee**a **pla**thas **lee**brays]

by the window/aisle — junto a las ventanillas/junto al pasillo [khoonto⌣a las vayntanee-yas/khoonto al pasee-yo]

smoking/non-smoking — para fumadores/no fumadores? [para foomadohrays/no foomadohrays]

* No quedan plazas libres. [no kaydan plathas leebrays] — Sorry, the flight is fully booked

How much is the ticket? — ¿Cuánto cuesta el pasaje? [kwanto kwaysta⌣ayl pasakhay]

Are there any special rates/ stand-by seats? — ¿Hay tarifas especiales/plazas stand-by? [aee tareefas ayspaytheealays/plathas standby]

When do I have to be at the airport? — ¿A qué hora tengo que estar en el aeropuerto? [a kay⌣ora tayngo kay⌣aystar ayn ayl ayropwayrto]

How much is the airport tax? — ¿Cuánto es la tasa de aeropuerto? [kwanto ays la tasa day⌣ayropwayrto]

My suitcase/My bag... — Mi maleta/Mi bolso... [mee malayta/mee bolso]
  has been damaged — está estropeada/-o [aysta⌣aystropayada/-o]
  is missing. — no está aquí [no⌣aysta⌣akee]

Getting around by boat

When does the next boat/(car) ferry leave for...? — ¿Cuándo hay un barco/un transbordador a...? [kwando⌣aee⌣oon barko/oon transbordador a]

How long does the crossing take? — ¿Cuánto tiempo dura la travesía? [kwanto teeaympo doora la travaysee a]

I'd like — **Quería** [kayreea]
  a ticket to... — un pasaje para... [oon pasakhay para]
    first class/tourist class — de primera/segunda clase [day preemayra/saygoonda klasay]

  a single/double cabin — un camarote individual/de dos camas [oon kamarotay⌣eendeeveedooal/day dos kamas]

  an outside/inside cabin — un camarote exterior/interior. [oon kamarotay extayreeor/⌣intayreeor]

I'd like to take the car with me. — Quería llevar el coche [kayreea yay-var el kochay]

When do I/we have to be on board? — ¿A qué hora tengo/tenemos que estar a bordo? [a kay⌣ora tayngo/taynaymos kay⌣aystar a bordo]

When do we arrive at...? — ¿A qué hora atracamos en...? [a kay⌣ora⌣atrakamos en]

How long are we stopping for? — ¿Cuánto tiempo nos quedamos? [kwanto teeaympo nos kaydamos]

I'm looking for — **Estoy buscando** [estoy booskando]
  cabin number... — el camarote número... [el kamarotay noomayro]

  the promenade deck — la cubierta (de paseo) [la koobeeayrta (de pasayo)]

  the parking deck — la cubierta de coches [la koobeeayrta day koches]

  a steward — un camarero [oon kamarayro]

The paradores are the jewel in the crown of the Spanish hotel industry. This luxury hotel in Carmona was once a palace owned by the Spanish king, Pedro

Accommodation

Hotels and guesthouses

Where can I find
a good/cheap/hotel in the centre of town

a guesthouse
close to the beach
in a quiet location?
Where is the... hotel/
guesthouse?

¿Hay por aquí [aee por‿akee]
un hotel bueno/no muy caro/céntrico
[oon o**tel** bwayno/no mwee **ka**ro/
thayntreeko]
una pensión [**oo**na payn**seeon**]
cerca de la playa [**thayr**ka day la **pla**-ya]
tranquilo/-a? [tran**kee**lo/-a]
¿Dónde está el hotel/la pensión...?
[**don**day‿ay**sta**‿ayl‿otayl/la payn**seeon**]

At the reception desk

I have a reservation.

My name is...

He reservado una habitación
[ay raysayr**va**do‿**oo**na‿abeeta**theeon**]
Me llamo... [may **ya**mo]

Have you got any vacancies

for one night
for one day/three days

for one week?
* Lo siento, pero estamos
completos [lo **seeayn**to
payro‿ay**sta**mos kom**play**tos]
* A partir del... hay cuartos
libres [a par**teer** dayl... aee
kwartos **lee**brays]

¿Hay una habitación libre
[aee‿**oo**na‿abeeta**theeon lee**bray]
para una noche [**para**‿**oo**na **no**chay]
para un día/para tres días
[**para**‿oon **dee**a/para trays **dee**as]
para una semana? [**para**‿**oo**na say**ma**na]
I'm afraid we're fully booked

There's a vacancy from...

I'd like/We'd like
a room with a shower

a single room

a double room
a room with twin beds

    with a bath and toilet
    with a balcony
    facing the beach/at the
      front

How much is the room

    per person
    per night
    per week
      with (without) breakfast
      with half board

      with full board?

Does the room have a
  television/telephone?

I'd like to see the room
This room is nice/is O.K.

I don't like this room

Do you have another room?

Quería/Queríamos [kayreea/kayreeamos]
una habitación con ducha
[oona‿abeetatheeon kon doocha]
un cuarto individual
[oon kwarto‿eendeeveedooal]
un cuarto doble [oon kwarto doblay]
un cuarto con dos camas
[oon kwarto kon dos kamas]
  con baño [kon ban-yo]
  con balcón [kon balkon]
  que dé a la playa/que dé a la calle
  [kay day a la pla-ya/kay day a la kayay]

¿Cuánto cuesta la habitación
[kwanto kwaysta la‿abeetatheeon]
  por persona [por payrsona]
  por noche [por nochay]
  por semana [por saymana]
  con (sin) desayuno [kon (sin) daysaeeoono]
  con media pensión [kon maydeea
  paynseeon]
  con pensión completa
  [kon paynseeon komplayta]
¿La habitación tiene televisión/teléfono?
[la‿abeetatheeon teeaynay taylayveeseeon/
taylayfono]
Quería ver el cuarto [kayreea bayr el kwarto]
El cuarto es bonito/está bien
[ayl kwarto‿ays boneeto/aysta beeayn]
El cuarto no me gusta [ayl kwarto no may
goosta]
¿Hay otro cuarto? [aee‿otro kwarto]

Accommodation

Visitors to Spain will find a wide variety of accommodation to choose from.

  Hoteles, which have a blue plate with a white H affixed to the facade, are placed in one of five categories according to the facilities offered and they given a star grading. At the very top of the range are the elite of the luxury hotels, the *gran lujo* category, of which there are only a handful throughout the country. The term *residencia* means that no meals are provided.

  Hostales (Hs) and *pensiones* (P) come into the mid-category range. They are smaller and more homely than *hoteles*, but do not usually have a restaurant and may not even serve breakfast. The cheaper hotels are called *fonda*, with a white F on a blue plate, and *casa de huespedes* (CH). Before checking in, it is advisable to have a quick look at the room on offer.

  If you want a Spanish experience to remember, then investigate the *paradores*. These state-run, upmarket hotels (of which there are about 75 on the Spanish mainland) often occupy historic buildings such as castles, country mansions and monasteries, and are located in especially attractive settings. These superior hotels are renowned for serving local gastronomic specialities.

Can I pay by cheque/credit card?	¿Puedo pagar con cheque/tarjeta de crédito? [**pway**do pa**gar** kon **chay**kay/tar**khay**ta day **kray**deeto]

Do you have
a car park
a (supervised) garage

a safe
a swimming-pool?

¿**Aquí tienen** [akee teeay**nayn**]
un aparcamiento [oon aparka**mee**ay**n**to]
un garaje (vigilado) [oon ga**rakhay** (beekhee**lado**)]
una caja fuerte [**oo**na **kakha** **fooayr**tay]
una piscina? [**oo**na pees**thee**na]

Where is
the breakfast room
the dining room?

¿**Dónde está** [donday_es**ta**]
la sala de desayuno [la **sala** day daysa**eeoo**no]
el comedor? [ayl komay**dor**]

What time is
breakfast
lunch
dinner?

¿**A qué hora sirven** [a kay_ora **seer**vayn]
el desayuno [ayl daysa**eeoo**no]
el almuerzo [ayl al**mooayr**tho]
la cena? [la **thay**na]

▶ **(Food and Drink, see page 40)**

Would you wake me
tomorrow at 7, please!

My key, please!
Room number 10, please!

¡Despiérteme mañana a las siete, por favor! [day**spee**ayr**tay**may man-**yana**_a las **seeay**tay por fa**vor**]

¡Mi llave, por favor! [mee **ya**-vay por fa**vor**]
¡Cuarto número diez, por favor! [**kwar**to **noo**mayro dee**ayth** por fa**vor**]

Where can I
change money
cash traveller's cheques

make a phone call?
Can I make a phone call to
England from my room?

Please put me through to
the following number... !

Are there any letters for me?

¿**Aquí puedo** [akee **pway**do]
cambiar dinero [kam**beear** dee**nay**ro]
cobrar cheques de viaje [ko**brar** **chay**kays day **beeakhay**]
telefonear? [taylayfona**yar**]
¿Puedo llamar desde mi cuarto a Inglaterra? [**pway**do ya**mar** **days**day mee **kwar**to_a_eenglatayra]
Póngame en comunicación con el número..., por favor [**pon**gamay_ayn komooneeka**theeon** kon ayl **noo**mayro... por fa**vor**]
¿Hay correo para mí? [aee ko**rayo** para_mee]

Complaints

The room is dirty/too loud

There's no (hot) water

El cuarto está sucio/es ruidoso [ayl **kwar**to_aysta soo**theeo**/ays rooee**do**so]
No tenemos agua (caliente) [no tay**nay**mos agooa (kaleeayntay)]

...does not work
The light
The shower
The toilet
The heating

...no funciona [no foonc**theeo**na]
La luz [la **looth**]
La ducha [la **doo**cha]
El lavabo [el la**va**bo]
La calefacción [la kalayfak**theeon**]

Hotel Reservation by Fax

Hotel Miramar
Alicante
Fax...

Señores:

Quería/Queríamos reservar una habitación para una persona/dos personas, si es posible un cuarto con ducha y balcón, desde el 1 hasta el 10 de agosto de 2001. Les ruego informarme/informarnos sobre los precios para cuartos individuales/dobles con desayuno/media pensión.

En espera de su confirmación, les saludamos atentamente,

Hotel Miramar
Alicante
Fax...

Dear Sir or Madam,

I/We would like to reserve a room from 1 to 10 August 2001 for one/two persons, if possible with shower and balcony.

Please let me/us know the price for a single/double room with breakfast/half-board and then confirm my/our booking as soon as possible.

Best wishes

There is/are no
  towels
  toilet paper

Falta/Faltan [falta/faltan]
  toallas [toa-yas]
  papel higiénico [papayl eekheeayneeko]

Could we have
  a blanket
  a pillow?
I've lost the key to my room

Necesitamos [naythayseetamos]
  una manta [oona manta]
  una almohada [oona_almoada]
He perdido la llave de mi cuarto
[ay payrdeedo la ya-vay day mee kwarto]

Departure

I'm leaving/We're leaving
  tomorrow/today
I'd like my bill, please
Could you call me a taxi, please
It's been very nice here

Parto/Partimos mañana/hoy
[parto/parteemos man-yana/oy]
La cuenta, por favor [la kwaynta por favor]
¡Llame un taxi, por favor!
[yamay_oon taxee por favor]
Nos ha gustado mucho estar aquí
[nos a goostado moocho_aystar akee]

Holiday cottages and holiday flats

We're looking for
  a holiday cottage/
  a holiday flat
  a (quiet) holiday flat

  for two/four people

  for six days/two weeks

How many rooms does the cottage have?

Buscamos [booskamos]
  una casa/un piso para las vacaciones
  [oona kasa/oon peeso para las vakatheeonays]
  un apartamento (tranquilo)
  [oon apartamaynto (trankeelo)]
  para dos/cuatro personas
  [para dos/kwatro payrsonas]
  para seis días/dos semanas
  [para sayees deeas/dos saymanas]
¿Cuántas habitaciones tiene la casa? [kwantas abeetatheeonays teeaynay la kasa]

ACCOMMODATION

How much is the flat/cottage?	¿Cuánto cuesta el piso/la casa? [**kwan**to **kway**sta el **pee**so/la **ka**sa]
Are there any additional costs?	¿Hay que pagar gastos adicionales? [aee kay pa**gar gas**tos adeetheeo**na**lays]
Are pets/dogs allowed?	¿Aceptan animales domésticos/perros? [a**thayp**tan anee**ma**lays do**may**steekos/**payr**ros]
Do we have to clean it before we leave?	¿Tenemos que hacer nosotros la limpieza final? [tay**nay**mos kay‿a**thayr** nos**o**tros la leem**pee**aytha fee**nal**]

Where can I
go shopping
make a phone call
do the laundry?

¿Dónde se puede [**don**day say **pway**day]
hacer compras [a**thayr kom**pras]
telefonear [taylayfona**yar**]
lavar ropa? [la**var ro**pa]

Camping

Have you got room for
a tent
a caravan
a camper van?

¿Hay sitio para [aee **see**teeo para]
una tienda [**oo**na tee**ayn**da]
una caravana [**oo**na kara**va**na]
una autocaravana? [**oo**na aooto kara**va**na]

What's the charge
for one person
for a car
for a camper van

for a caravan
for a tent?

¿Cuánto cuesta [**kwan**to **kway**sta]
por persona [por **payr**sona]
para un coche [para‿**oon ko**chay]
para una autocaravana
[para‿**oo**na aooto kara**va**na]
para una caravana [para‿**oo**na kara**va**na]
para una tienda? [para‿**oo**na tee**ayn**da]

Do you also rent out
caravans
bungalows/cabins?
Where are the showers/toilets?

¿Se alquilan también [say‿al**kee**lan tam**bee**ayn]
caravanas [kara**va**nas]
chalés/cabañas? [cha**lays**/ka**ban**-yas]
¿Dónde están las duchas/los lavabos?
[**don**day‿ay**stan** las **doo**chas/los la**va**bos]

We need
a power point

a tap for water
When is the gate locked at night?
Is the camp-site guarded at night?

Necesitamos [naythaysee**ta**mos]
electricidad/toma de corriente
[aylayktreethee**da**/**to**ma day korree**ayn**tay]
un grifo de agua [**gree**fo day‿**a**gooa]
¿Cuándo cierran la puerta por la noche?
[**kwan**do thee**ay**rran la **pwayr**ta por la **no**chay]
¿El camping está vigilado durante la noche?
[el **kam**peeng ay**sta** beekhee**la**do du**ran**tay la **no**chay]

Does the camp-site have
a supermarket
a restaurant
public washing machines
cool boxes
a playground?

¿En el camping hay [ayn ayl **kam**peeng aee]
un supermercado [oon soopermayr**ka**do]
un restaurante [oon raystaoo**ran**tay]
lavadoras [lava**do**ras]
neveras [nay**vay**ras]
un parque de juegos infantiles?
[oon **par**kay day **khoo**aygos eenfan**tee**lays]

Youth hostel

Is there a youth hostel near here?	¿Hay un albergue juvenil por aquí? [aee_oon albayrgay khoobayneel por_akee]
How much is it per night	¿Cuánto cuesta una noche? [kwanto kwaysta_oona nochay]
per person (with breakfast)?	por persona (con desayuno)? [por payrsona (kon daysaeeoono)]
We have a reservation	Hemos hecho una reserva [aymos aycho oona raysayrva]
Do you have a family room?	¿Tienen una habitación para familias? [teeaynayn oona abeetatheeon para fameeleeas]

Accommodation

adapter	adaptador (m) [adaptador]
air conditioning	aire (m) acondicionado [aeeray_akondeetheeonado]
apartment	apartamento [apartamaynto]
ashtray	cenicero [thayneethayro]
balcony	balcón (m) [balkon]
bathtub	bañera [baneeayra]
bed	cama [kama]
bed-linen	ropa de cama [ropa day kama]
bill	cuenta [kooenta]
blanket	colcha [kolcha]
bottled gas	bombona de gas [bombona day gas]
camper van	autocaravana [aootokaravana]
caravan	caravana [karavana]
car park	aparcamiento [aparkameeaynto]
chamber maid	camarera [kamarayra]
clean	limpiar [leempeear]
coins	monedas [monaydas]
cooker (electric/gas)	cocina (eléctrica/de gas) [kotheena (aylayktreeka/day gas)]
cot	cama de niños [kama day neenyos]
coat-hanger	percha [payrcha]
crockery	vajilla [bakhee-ya]
dining room	comedor (m) [komaydor]
drinking water	agua potable [agooa potablay]
extra costs	gastos adicionales [gastos adeetheeonalays]
family room	habitación (f) para familias [abeetatheeon para fameeleeas]
fan	ventilador [baynteelador]
final cleaning	limpieza final [leempeeaytha feenal]
garage	garaje (m) [garakhay]
guesthouse	pensión (f) [paynseeon]

I/We will stay for two days/ weeks	Me quedo/Nos quedamos dos días/semanas [may **kay**do/nos kay**da**mos dos **dee**as/ say**ma**nas]
I need/I don't need bed-linen	(No) Necesito ropa de cama [(no) naythay**see**to **ro**pa day **ka**ma]
When is the front door locked?	¿A qué hora cierran la puerta de entrada? [a kay⌣ora thee**ay**ran la **pwayr**ta day⌣ayn**tra**da]

How far is it to
  the beach
  the town centre
  the station?

¿Está lejos [esta **lay**khos]
  la playa [la **pla**–ya]
  la ciudad [la theeoo**dad**]
  la estación? [la⌣aysta**theeon**]

heating	calefacción *(f)* [kalayfak**theeon**]
hire/borrow	alquilar [alkee**lar**]
hire charge	tarifa de alquiler [ta**ree**fa day⌣alkee**layr**]
key	llave *(f)* [**ya**vay]
kitchen	cocina [ko**thee**na]
lift	ascensor *(m)* [asthayn**sor**]
light	luz *(f)* [looth]
luggage	equipaje *(m)* [aykee**pa**khay]
pillow	almohada [almo-**a**da]
pots	ollas [**o**yas]
power (point)	(toma de) electricidad [(**to**ma day) aylayktreethee**dad**]
reduction	reducción *(f)* [raydook**theeon**]
repair	reparar [raypa**rar**]
rubbish (bin)	(cubo de) basura [(**koo**bo daay) ba**soo**ra]
safe	caja fuerte [**ka**kha **fooayr**tay]
shower	ducha [**doo**cha]
sink	lavabo [la**va**bo]
sleeping bag	saco de dormir [**sa**ko day dor**meer**]
soap	jabón *(m)* [kha**bon**]
sports ground	campo de deportes [**kam**po day day**por**tays]
tea towel	paño de cocina [**pan**yo day ko**thee**na]
telephone	teléfono [tay**lay**fono]
television	televisión *(m)* [taylayvee**sion**]
tent peg	piquete *(m)* [pee**kay**tay]
toilet paper	papel *(m)* higiénico [pa**payl** eekhee**ay**neeko]
toilets	lavabos/aseos/servicios [la**va**bos/a**say**os/sayr**bee**theeos]
towel	toalla [to-**a**ya]
wash/washing machine	lavar/lavadora [la**var**/lava**do**ra](gastos del)
water (consumption)	agua [(**gas**tos del) a**goo**a]

Paella, *a rice dish with a reputation that now extends way beyond the Valencia region*

Food and Drink

Is there... around here?
a good/a reasonably cheap restaurant
a nice/a typical restaurant

with regional/ international cuisine?

¿Dónde hay por aquí [donday‿aee por‿akee]
un restaurante bueno/no muy caro
[oon raystaoorantay **bway**no/no mwee **ka**ro]
un restaurante acogedor/típico
[oon raystaoorantay‿akokhay**dor/tee**peeko]
de cocina regional/internacional?
[day ko**thee**na raykheeo**nal**/eenternatheeo**nal**]

I'd like/We'd like
to have breakfast
to have lunch
to have dinner
a snack
just something to drink.

Quería/Queríamos [kay**ree**a/kay**ree**amos]
desayunar [daysayoo**nar**]
almorzar [almor**thar**]
cenar [thay**nar**]
picar algo [pee**kar**‿algo]
sólo beber algo [**so**lo bay**bayr**‿algo]

I'd like to reserve a table

for tonight/tomorrow night

at 7/8 o'clock

for 4/6 persons.

The name is...
I've reserved a table. The name is...
A table for 2/4, please!

Is this table/seat taken?

Quería reservar una mesa
[kay**ree**a raysayr**var** oona **may**sa]
para hoy/para mañana por la noche
[para‿oy/para ma**nya**na por la **no**chay]
a las siete/ocho de la tarde
[a las deeaythee**nooay**bay/be-ee**n**tay‿**oh**ras]
para cuatro/seis personas
[para **kwa**tro/say-ees payr**so**nas]
a nombre de... [a **nom**bray day]
He reservado una mesa a nombre de...
[e raysayr**va**do oona **may**sa‿a **nom**bray day]
Una mesa para dos/cuatro personas, por favor.
[oona **may**sa para dos/**kwa**tro payr**so**nas por fa**vor**]
¿Esta mesa/Este asiento está libre?
[**ays**ta **may**sa/**es**tay a**see**aynto‿**es**ta **lee**bray]

Do you have high chairs? ¿Tienen sillas altas para niños?
[teeaynayn see-yas altas para neen-yos]

Excuse me, where's the toilet? ¿Dónde están los lavabos, por favor?
[donday⌣aystan los lavabos por favor]

How to order

Excuse me, please! ¡Por favor!/¡Oiga, por favor!
[por favor/oeega por favor]

The menu, please! ¡La carta/El menú! [la karta/el menu]

The wine list, please! La carta de vinos, por favor
[la karta day beenos por favor]

* ¿Qué desean?/¿Qué van a What would you like/What are you going to
tomar? [kay daysayan/kay have?
van⌣a tomar]

What would you recommend? ¿Qué me recomienda? [kay may
raykomeeaynda]

I'll have **Quería/Tomo** [kayreea/tomo]

soup una sopa [oona sopa]

the dish of the day el plato del día [el plato del deea]

menu number 1/2 el menú número uno/dos
[el maynoo noomayro⌣oono/dos]

this esto [aysto]

as a starter/as the main de primero/de segundo/de postre
course/for dessert. [day preemayro/day saygoondo/day postray]

Do you have any regional ¿Cuáles son los platos típicos de esta región?
specialities? [kwalays son los platos teepeekos day⌣aysta
raykheeon]

Could I have rice instead of Prefiero arroz en vez de patatas fritas
chips, please? [prayfeeayro⌣arroth ayn bayth day patatas freetas]

The Spanish daily timetable

The Spanish daily rhythm is quite different to that of northern Europe. Many Spaniards dash out of the house as soon as they wake up, dispensing with breakfast. They prefer to have a cup of coffee and a sweet pastry such as a doughnut, a little cake, chocolate-filled croissants, *churros* (delicious sugar-coated batter pieces) or *ensaimadas* (pastries filled with tuna, meat or cheese), as a mid-morning snack.

Lunch (*almuerzo*) is taken at about 2pm at home and between 1.30 and 3.30pm in restaurants. This is almost always a family gathering around the table. The lunch break lasts for about two hours and many people will, if possible, have a nap (*siesta*).

In most families, supper (*cena*) will not begin until 8pm at the earliest. After supper, it's time to head out to a bar or the cinema, or just for an evening stroll. The Spanish tend to stay out often well beyond midnight.

A Spanish pub-crawl or *copeo* will start with a *café solo* in the bar around the corner from home. Then it's on to the nearest *bodega* or *cervecería*, or perhaps to a trendy bar with music (*pub*).

Spanish discos (*discotecas*) don't start swinging until after midnight. The night draws to a close in the early hours in a *churrería*, a cake shop or kiosk selling *churros* dipped in thick hot chocolate.

FOOD AND DRINK

For the child/children

a small portion

an extra plate
extra cutlery, please.

Do you have a vegetarian
dish?
Is this dish (very) hot/sweet/
rich?

* ¿Y para beber?
[ee para baybayr]

**For me/For the lady/
For the gentleman**
a beer
a mineral water

To drink I'd like/we'd like

a glass
a bottle
a quarter of a litre
half a litre/one litre of
red wine/white wine,
please
We'll have the house wine/a
table wine

* ¿Desean algo más?
[daysayan algo mas]
No, thank you, that's all

Could I have... please?
some more bread
another beer
Enjoy your meal!

Cheers!/Your health!
Do you mind if I smoke?

Para el niño/los niños [para‿ayl neenyo/los neenyos]
una ración pequeña [oona ratheeon paykaynya]
un plato extra [oon plato ayxtra]
un cubierto, por favor [oon kubeeayrto por favor]
¿Hay un plato vegetariano?
[aee oon plato baykhaytareeano]
¿Este plato es (muy) picante/dulce/grasiento?
[aystay plato ays (mwee) peekántay/doolthay/graseeaynto]
What would you like to drink?

Para mí/Para la señora/Para el señor
[para‿mee/para‿la saynyora/para‿el saynyor]
una cerveza [oona thayrbaytha]
un agua mineral [oon‿agooa meenayral]

Para beber quería/queríamos
[para baybayr kayreea/kayreeamos]
una copa [oona kopa]
una botella [oona botay-ya]
un cuarto de litro [oon kwarto day leetro]
medio/un litro [maydeeo/oon leetro]
de vino tinto/vino blanco, por favor
[day beeno teento/beeno blanko por favor]
Tomamos el vino de la casa/un vino de mesa
[tomamos el beeno day la kasa/oon beeno day maysa]
Would you like anything else?

No gracias, es todo
[no gratheeas, es todo]

¿Me puede traer... [may pwayday tra-ayr]
más pan [mas pan]
otra cerveza? [otra thayrbaytha]
¡Buen provecho!/¡Que aproveche!
[bwayn probaycho/kay‿aprobaychay]
¡Salud! [salood]
¿Puedo fumar? [pwaydo foomar]

Complaints

That's not what I ordered!

Have you forgotten
my food
my drink?

¡Yo no he pedido eso! [yo no ay paydeedo‿ayso]

¿Se ha olvidado [say‿a‿olbeedado]
de mi plato [day mee plato]
de mi bebida? [day mee baybeeda]

We still need..., please?
some cutlery
another knife
another fork
another spoon/another
teaspoon
another plate
another glass

Falta [falta]
un cubierto [oon koobeeayrto]
un cuchillo [oon koochee-yo]
un tenedor [oon taynaydor]
una cuchara/una cucharita
[oona koochara/oona koochareeta]
un plato [oon plato]
(water) un vaso; *(wine)* una copa
[oon baso/oona kopa]

Could we have..., please?
oil and vinegar
salt and pepper
napkins
toothpicks
an ashtray

¡Tráiganos por favor¡... [traeeganos por favor]
aceite y vinagre [athayeetay‿ee veenagray]
sal y pimienta [sal ee peemeeaynta]
unas servilletas [oonas sayrvee-yaytas)
unos palillos [oonos palee-yos]
un cenicero [oon thayneethayro]

I'm sorry but
the soup/the food is cold

the meat is tough/not
cooked through.

There seems to be a mistake
in the bill
What is this, please?
I didn't have that!

Lo siento, pero [lo seeaynto payro]
la sopa/la comida está fría
[la sopa/la komeeda‿aysta freea]
la carne está dura/no está bien pasada
[la karnay‿aysta doora/no‿aysta beeayn
pasada]
Creo que la cuenta no está correcta.
[krayo kay la kooaynta no‿aysta koraykta]
¿Qué es esto? [kay‿es esto]
¡Yo no he tomado eso! [yo no‿ay tomado‿ayso]

Paying the bill

Could I have the bill, please!
All together, please
Separate bills, please

Could I have a receipt,
please?

¡La cuenta, por favor! [la kooaynta por favor]
Pago todo junto [pago todo khoonto]
¡Cuentas separadas por favor!
[kooayntas sayparadas por favor]
¿Me da un recibo, por favor?
[may‿da‿oon raytheevo por favor]

* ¿Le *(sing)*/Les *(pl)* ha
gustado la comida?
[le/les a gustado la komeeda]
It was very good, thank you
That's for you
Keep the change!

Did you enjoy the meal?

Sí, estaba muy rica [see aystaba mwee reeka]
Para usted [para‿ustayd]
Está bien así [aysta beeayn asee]

Paying the bill

If you go to a restaurant with friends
while you're in Spain, do not expect the
waiter to divide up the bill individually
for each of you. Either one of the party
agrees to pay the total in full or every-
body contributes their respective share
of the bill.
The tip *(propina)* – generally about
10 percent of the whole bill – is simply
left on the table.

43

Food

Desayuno	Breakfast
café *(m)* [ka**fay**]	coffee
con leche *(f)* [kon **lay**chay]	with milk
con azúcar *(m)* [kon a**thoo**kar]	with sugar
con sacarina [kon saka**ree**na]	with sweetener
cortado [kor**ta**do]	small coffee with milk
descafeinado [dayskafay-ee**na**do]	decaffeinated
solo [**so**loh]	black
chocolate *(m)* [choko**la**tay]	hot chocolate
croissant *(m)* [kroa**sant**]	croissant
embutido [aymboo**tee**do]	cold meats
huevo frito [**ooay**bo **free**to]	fried egg
huevo pasado por agua	soft boiled egg
[**ooay**bo pa**sa**do por_**a**gooa]	
huevo revuelto [**ooay**bo ray**vooayl**to]	scrambled egg
con jamón [kon kha**mon**]	with ham
infusión *(f)* [eenfoo**seeon**]	herbal tea
jamón *(m)* serrano [kha**mon** say**ra**no]	smoked ham
jamón *(m)* York [kha**mon** york]	cooked ham
leche *(f)* (caliente/fría)	(hot/cold) milk
[**lay**chay (kaleeayn**tay**/**free**a)]	
mantequilla [manta**kee**-ya]	butter
margarina [marga**ree**na]	margarine
mermelada [mayrmay**la**da]	jam
miel *(f)* [**mee**ayl]	honey
pan *(m)* [pan]	bread
pan *(m)* integral [pan eentay**gral**]	wholemeal bread
panecillo [pana**thee**-yo]	bread roll
queso [**kay**so]	cheese
té *(m)* (con limón) [tay (kon lee**mon**)]	tea (with lemon)
tortilla [tor**tee**-ya]	omelette
yogur *(m)* [yo**gur**]	yogurt
natural/de fruta [natoo**ral**/day **froo**ta]	natural/with fruit
zumo de naranja [**thoo**mo day na**ran**kha]	orange juice

Snacks	Snacks
bocadillo/sandwich *(m)*	bread roll/sandwich
[boka**dee**-yo/**san**weech]	
de jamón *(m)* (York) [day kha**mon** (york)]	with (cooked) ham
de jamón *(m)* serrano [day kha**mon** say**ra**no]	with cured ham
de queso/salchicha [day **kay**so/sal**chee**cha]	with cheese/sausage
de salchichón [day salchee**chon**]	with salami
hamburguesa [amboor**gooay**sa]	hamburger
patatas fritas [pa**ta**tas **free**tas]	chips/french fries
con ketchup [kon **kay**choop]	with ketchup
con mayonesa [kon maeeo**nay**sa]	with mayonnaise
perro caliente [**pay**ro kalee**ayn**tay]	hot dog
tortilla [tor**tee**-ya]	omelette
de patatas [day pa**ta**tas]	Spanish potato omelette

Entremeses/Tapas	**Starters**
aceitunas [athay-eetoonas]	olives
verdes/negras [bayrdays/naygras]	green/black
albóndigas [albondeegas]	meatballs
almejas [almaykhas]	clams
almendras [almayndras]	almonds
boquerones [bokayronays]	fresh anchovies
champiñones rellenos	stuffed mushrooms
[champeeneeonays ray-aynos]	
chorizo [choreetho]	spicy sausage
gambas (al ajillo) [gambas (al akhee-yo)]	prawns (in garlic oil)
pinchos [peenchos]	spicy meat kebabs
salpicón (m) de marisco	seafood salad
[salpeekon day mareesko]	
fritos [freetos]	deep fried
en vinagre [en‿beenagray]	in vinegar and oil
Sopas	**Soups**
caldo [kaldo]	clear soup
gazpacho (andaluz) [gathpacho (andalooth)]	cold tomato and garlic soup
sopa de ajo [sopa day‿akho]	garlic soup
sopa de almendras [sopa day‿almayndras]	almond soup
sopa de fideos [sopa day feedayos]	noodle soup
sopa de mariscos [sopa day mareeskos]	seafood soup
sopa de pescado [sopa day payskado]	fish soup
sopa juliana [sopa khooleeana]	vegetable soup
Pescados y mariscos	**Fish and seafood**
almejas [almaykhas]	clams
anguila [angeela]	eel
angulas [angoolas]	elver
arenque (m) [araynkay]	herring
atún [atoon]	tuna
bacalao [bakalao]	cod
besugo [baysoogo]	bream
bogavante (m) [bogabantay]	lobster
caballa [kaba-ya]	mackerel
calamares [kalamarays]	squid
en su tinta [en soo teenta)]	cooked in its ink
cangrejo [kangraykho]	crab
carpa [karpa]	carp
dorada [dorada]	sea bream
gambas [gambas]	prawns
langostinos [langosteenos]	king prawns
lenguado [layngooado]	sole
mejillones [maykhee-yonays]	mussels
merluza [mayrlootha]	hake
ostras [ostras]	oysters
paella (valenciana) [pa-ay-a (balaynthyana)]	rice with seafood
parrillada de pescado	platter of grilled fish
[paree-yada day payskado]	

pescadilla [payskadee-ya)	baby hake
pez espada [payth ayspada]	swordfish
pulpo [**pool**po]	(giant) squid
rape *(m)* [**ra**pay]	angler-fish
salmón *(m)* [sal**mon**]	salmon
sardinas [sar**dee**nas]	sardines
trucha [**troo**cha]	trout
vieiras [bee-ay-eeras]	scallops
zarzuela de marisco/pescado [thar**thooay**la day mareesko/payskado]	seafood/fish stew

Carne — **Meat**

asado [a**sa**do]	roast
bistec *(m)* [bee**stayk**]	beef steak
cabrito [ka**bree**to]	kid
callos [**ka**-yos]	tripe
carne *(f)* [**kar**nay]	meat
de cerdo [day **thayr**do]	pork
de vaca [day **ba**ka]	beef
picada [pee**ka**da]	minced meat
cazuela de lentejas [ka**thooay**la day layn**tay**khas]	spicy sausage and lentil stew
chorizo [cho**ree**tho]	spicy sausage
chuleta [choo**lay**ta]	chop
cocido [ko**thee**do]	meat, vegetable and chickpea stew
cochinillo [kochee**nee**yo]	suckling pig
conejo [ko**nay**kho]	rabbit
cordero [kor**day**ro]	lamb/mutton
empanada [aympa**na**da]	(meat-)pie
escalope *(m)* [ayska**lo**pay]	escalope
a la milanesa [a la meela**nay**sa]	breaded
estofado [esto**fa**do]	stewed meat
fabada asturiana [fa**ba**da astooree**a**na]	meat and bean casserole
filete *(m)* [fee**lay**tay]	fillet steak
a la inglesa [a la eeng**lay**sa]	medium-rare
bien pasado [beeayn pa**sa**do]	well-done
poco pasado [**po**ko pa**sa**do]	medium
hígado [**ee**gado]	liver
lomo de ternera [**lo**mo day tayr**nay**ra]	sirloin
lomo de corzo [**lo**mo day **kor**tho]	saddle of venison
parrillada de carne [paree-**ya**da day karnay]	mixed grill
pierna de cordero [**peeayr**na day kor**day**ro]	leg of lamb
pinchos [**peen**chos]	kebabs
rosbif *(m)* [**ros**beef]	roast beef
solomillo [solo**mee**yo]	fillet/loin
ternera [tayr**nay**ra]	veal

Aves — **Poultry**

codorniz *(f)* [kodor**neeth**]	quail
faisán *(m)* [faee**san**]	pheasant

46

pato [**pa**to]
pavo [**pa**bo]
pechuga de pollo [pay**choo**ga day **po**-yo]
pollo [**po**-yo]

duck
turkey
chicken breast
chicken

Plato Adicionál/Guarnición
arroz [a**roth**]
croquetas [kro**kay**tas]
macarrones [maka**ro**nays]
pan/panecillos [pan/panay**thee**-yos]
pastas [**pas**tas]
patatas [pa**ta**tas]
patatas fritas [pa**ta**tas **free**tas]

Side dishes
rice
croquettes
macaroni
bread/bread rolls
pasta
potatoes
chips/french fries

Ensalada y Verduras
alcachofas [alka**cho**fas]
berenjenas [bayrayn**khay**nas]
brócoli *(m)* [**bro**kolee]
calabacines *(m)* [kalaba**thee**nays]
cebolla [thay**bo**-ya]
coliflor *(m)* [kolee**flor**]
ensalada (mixta) [ayn**sa**lada (**meex**ta)]
espárragos [ay**spa**ragos]
espinacas [ayspee**na**kas]
guisantes *(m)* [gooee**san**tays]
judías blancas [khoo**dee**as **blan**kas]
judías verdes [khoo**dee**as **bayr**days]
lechuga [lay**choo**ga]
lentejas [layn**tay**khas]
pepino [pay**pee**no]
pimiento [pee**meeayn**to]
pisto manchego [**pees**to man**chay**go]

champiñones/setas [champeen-**yo**nays/**say**tas]

Salads and vegetables
artichokes
aubergines/eggplant
broccoli
courgettes
onion
cauliflower
(mixed) salad
asparagus
spinach
peas
haricot beans
runner beans
lettuce
lentils
cucumber
sweet pepper
vegetable casserole
from Mancha
mushrooms

Quesos
manchego [man**chay**go]
queso azul [**kay**so‿a**thool**]
queso de cabra [**kay**so day **ka**bra]
queso de oveja [**kay**so day‿o**bay**kha]
requesón [raykay**son**]

Cheese
sheep's cheese from Mancha
blue cheese
goat's cheese
sheep's cheese
cream cheese/cottage cheese

Postres/Dulces
churros [**choo**ros]
crema catalana [**kray**ma kata**la**na]
flan *(m)* [flan]
macedonia [mathay**do**neea]
natillas [na**tee**-yas]
tarta de manzanas [**tar**ta day man**tha**nas]
tocino de cielo [to**thee**no day **theeay**lo]

Desserts
deep fried doughnut
vanilla and egg custard
creme caramel
fruit salad
custard
apple tart
sweet dish made of
sugar and egg yolks

torta de almendras [**tor**ta day＿al**mayn**dras]   almond tart
turrón *(m)* [too**ron**]   almond nougat
▶ (**Fruit**, *see shopping, page 62*)

Helados   **Ice Cream**
helado [ay**la**do]   ice cream
   de chocolate [day choko**la**tay]   chocolate
   de fresa [day **fray**sa]   strawberry
   de limón [day lee**mon**]   lemon
   de nuez [day noo**ayth**]   walnut
   de vainilla [day baee**nee**ya]   vanilla
helado variado [ay**la**do ba**ree**ado]   mixed ice cream
   con frutas [kon **froo**tas]   with fruit
   con nata [kon **na**ta]   with cream

Drinks

Bebidas alcohólicas   **Alcoholic drinks**
aguardiente *(m)* [agooar**deeayn**tay]   various strong liquors
aperitivo [apayree**tee**bo]   apéritif
caña [**ka**nya]   small beer
cava *(m)* [**ka**va]   sparkling wine
cerveza (de barril) [thayr**bay**tha (day ba**reel**)]   (draught) beer
champán *(m)* [cham**pan**]   champagne
ginebra [khee**nay**bra]   gin
jerez *(m)* [khay**rayth**]   sherry
Málaga *(m)* [**ma**laga]   dessert wine
moscatel *(m)* [moska**tayl**]   muscat wine
ponche *(m)* [**pon**chay]   punch
ron *(m)* [ron]   rum
sangría [san**gree**a]   red wine and fruit punch
vino [**bee**no]   wine
   blanco [**blan**ko]   white wine
   rosado [ro**sa**do]   rosé wine
   tinto [**teen**to]   red wine
     dulce [**dool**thay]   sweet
     seco/semiseco [**say**ko/saymee**say**ko]   dry/medium dry

Refrescos   **Soft drinks**
agua mineral [**a**gooa meenay**ral**]   mineral water
   con/sin gas [kon/seen gas]   sparkling/still
batido de leche [ba**tee**do day **lay**chay]   milkshake
gaseosa [gasay-**o**sa]   fizzy drink
horchata [or**cha**ta]   almond milk
limonada [leemo**na**da]   lemonade
naranjada [naran**kha**da]   orangeade
tónica [**to**neeka]   tonic water
zumo de fruta [**thoo**mo day **froo**ta]   fruit juice
zumo de naranja [**thoo**mo day naran**kha**]   orange juice
▶ (**Hot drinks**, *see breakfast, page 44.*)

Bullfighting (corrida de toros) takes place between Easter and October. This bullring in Mijas is one of many in Andalusia

Sightseeing

Tourist information

Is there/Are there
a tourist office

an information office?
guided tours?
sightseeing tours of the city?

¿Hay por aquí [aee por‿akee]
una oficina de turismo?
[oona‿ofee**thee**na day too**ree**smo]
una información? [oona‿eenforma**theeon**]
visitas guiadas? [bee**see**tas gee**a**das]
excursiones? [exkoor**see**onays]

Do you have
a street map?

a map of the city centre/ the area?

a map of the underground?
brochures?
a list of hotels?

a list of restaurants?

a programme of events?

for this week/for the festival?
Could you book a room for me?
What are the places of interest around here?

¿Tiene usted [tee**ay**nay‿**oo**stay]
un plano de la ciudad?
[oon **pla**no day la thee**oo**da]
un mapa del centro/de los alrededores?
[oon **ma**pa del **thayn**tro/day los alrayday**do**rays]
un plano del metro? [oon **pla**no del **may**tro]
folletos? [fo**yay**tos]
una lista de hoteles?
[**oo**na **lee**sta day‿o**tay**lays]
una lista de restaurantes?
[**oo**na **lee**sta day raysta-oo**ran**tays]
un calendario de actos?
[oon kalayn**da**reeo day‿**ak**tos]
para esta semana/para la(s) fiesta(s)?
[**pa**ra **ay**sta say**ma**na/**pa**ra la(s) **feeay**sta(s)]
¿Me puede reservar un cuarto?
[may **pway**day raysayr**var** oon **kwar**to]
¿Qué monumentos hay para visitar aquí?
[kay monoo**mayn**tos aee **pa**ra veesee**tar** a**kee**]

49

Sightseeing

altar	altar *(m)* [al**tar**]
amphitheatre	anfiteatro [anfeetay**a**tro]
ancient	antiguo [an**tee**goo-o]
architecture	arquitectura [arkeetayk**too**ra]
arena	arena [a**ray**na]
art	arte *(f)* [**ar**tay]
artist	artista *(m/f)* [ar**tee**sta]
arts and crafts	artesanato [artaysa**na**to]
baroque	barroco [ba**ro**ko]
basilica	basílica [ba**see**leeka]
botanical gardens	jardín *(m)* botánico [khar**deen** bo**ta**neeko]
bridge	puente *(m)* [**pway**ntay]
building	edificio [aydee**fee**theeo]
bull ring	plaza de toros [**pla**tha day **to**ros]
castle	castillo [kas**tee**-yo]
cave	cueva [**koo**ayba]
Celtic	céltico [**thayl**teeko]
cemetery	cementerio [thaymayn**tay**reeo]
century	siglo [**see**glo]
ceramics	cerámica [thay**ra**meeka]
chapel	capilla [ka**pee**-ya]
Christian	cristiano [krees**tee**ano]
copy	copia [**ko**peea]
cross	cruz *(f)* [krooth]
emperor	emperador [aympayra**dor**]
empress	emperatriz [aympayra**treeth**]
epoch	época [**ay**poka]
excavations	excavaciones *(f)* [ayxkava**thee**onays]
facade	fachada [fa**cha**da]
forest	bosque *(m)* [**bos**kay]
fortress	fortaleza/ciudadela [forta**lay**tha/theeooda**day**la]
gallery	galería [galay**ree**a]
garden	jardín *(m)* [khar**deen**]
gate	puerta [poo**ayr**ta]
glass (pane of)	vidrio/cristál *(m)* [**bee**dreeo/krees**tal**]
gorge	barranco [ba**ran**ko]
gothic	gótico [**go**teeko]
(tourist) guide	guía (m/f) [**gee**a]
inscription	inscripción *(f)* [eenskreep**theeon**]
island	isla [**ees**la]
king	rey [rayee]
lake	lago [**la**go]
landscape	paisaje *(m)* [paeesa**khay**]
lane	callejón *(m)* [ka-yay**khon**]
library	biblioteca [beebleeo**tay**ka]

lookout point	mirador *(m)* [meera**dor**]
market	mercado [mayr**ka**do]
medieval	medieval [maydeeay**val**]
memorial	monumento [monoo**mayn**to]
monastery/convent	monasterio/convento [mona**stay**reeo/kon**vayn**to]
monument	monumento [monoo**mayn**to]
moorish	moro [**mo**ro]
mosque	mezquita [meth**kee**ta]
mountain	montaña [mon**ta**nya]
nature reserve	reserva natural/reserva ecológica [ray**sayr**ba natoo**ral**/ray**sayr**ba‿aykolo**lo**kheeka]
old town	centro histórico [**thayn**tro‿ee**sto**reeko]
organ	órgano [**or**gano]
original	original *(m)* [oreekhee**nal**]
painter	pintora [peen**to**ra]
painting	pintura [peen**too**ra]
panorama	panorama [pano**ra**ma]
park	parque *(m)* [**par**kay]
picture	cuadro/pintura [**kwa**dro/peen**too**ra]
port	puerto [pw**ayr**to]
prehistoric	prehistórico [prayee**sto**reeko]
queen	reina [**rayee**na]
relief	relieve *(m)* [ray**leeay**vay]
Renaissance	Renacimiento [raynathee**meeayn**to]
Romanesque	románico [ro**ma**neeko]
roof	techo [**tay**cho]
ruin	ruina [roo**ee**na]
sculpture	escultura [ayskool**too**ra]
square	plaza [**pla**tha]
statue	estatua [ay**sta**tooa]
style	estilo [ay**stee**lo]
synagogue	sinagoga [seena**go**ga]
temple	templo [**taym**plo]
theatre	teatro [tay**a**tro]
tomb	tumba/sepulcro [**toom**ba/say**pool**kro]
tower	torre *(f)* [**to**ray]
town hall	ayuntamiento [a-yoonta**meeayn**to]
town wall	muralla [moo**ra‑**ya]
valley	valle *(m)* [**ba**yay]
view	vista [**vee**sta]
vineyard	bodega [bo**day**ga]
waterfall	cascada [ka**ska**da]
yard	patio [**pa**teeo]
zoo	parque zoológico [**par**kay thoo**lo**kheekho]

51

Visiting the sights

I'd like/We'd like to visit

Quería/Queríamos visitar
[kay**ree**a/kay**ree**amos veese**tar**]

the cathedral
la catedral [la katay**dral**]

the church
la iglesia [la⌣ee**glay**seea]

the palace
el palacio [ayl pa**la**theeo]

the castle
el castillo [ayl ka**stee**yo]

What are the opening hours of the exhibition?
¿Cuándo está abierta la exposición? [**kwan**do⌣ay**sta**⌣a**bee**ayrta la⌣ayxposee**theeon**]

When does the museum close?
¿Cuándo cierra el museo? [**kwan**do **thee**ayra⌣ayl moo**say**o]

Is there a guided tour in English?
¿Hay una visita guiada en inglés? [aee⌣**oo**na vee**see**ta gee**a**da ayn een**glays**]

When does it start?
¿Cuándo empieza? [**kwan**do⌣aym**pee**aytha]

How much is it?
¿Cuánto cuesta? [**kwan**to **kway**sta]

How long does it take?
¿Cuánto tiempo dura? [**kwan**to tee**aym**po **doo**ra]

One/Two ticket(s) for adults/children, please.
Una/Dos entrada para adultos/niños, por favor [**oo**na/dos ayn**tra**da **pa**ra⌣a**dool**tos/**nee**nyos por fa**vor**]

Are there special rates for children/students/senior citizens?
¿Hay un descuento para niños/estudiantes/la tercera edad? [aee⌣oon days**kooayn**to **pa**ra **nee**nyos/estoo**dee**antays/la tayr**thay**ra⌣ay**dad**]

* ¡Prohibido fotografiar!
[proee**bee**do fotogra**feear**]

No cameras allowed!

Can I use my video camera?
¿Puedo filmar aquí? [**pway**do feel**mar** a**kee**]

Do you have a catalogue/ guide in English?
¿Tiene un catálogo/una guía en inglés? [tee**ay**nay oon ka**ta**logo/**oo**na **gee**a ayn een**glays**]

Excursions

How much is the excursion to...?
¿Cuánto cuesta la excursión a...? [**kwan**to **kway**sta la⌣ayxkoor**seeon** a]

Do we have to pay extra for the meal/for admission charges?
¿Hay que pagar la comida/las entradas aparte? [aee kay pa**gar** la ko**mee**da/las ayn**tra**das a**par**tay]

Two tickets for... excursion, please.

Dos billetes para la excursión a...
[dos bee**yay**tays **pa**ra la⌣ayxkoor**seeon** a]

today's/tomorrow's/the 10 o'clock
hoy/mañana/a las diez [oy/man**ya**na/a las dee**ayth**]

When/Where do we meet?
¿A qué hora/Dónde nos encontramos? [a kay⌣**o**ra/**don**day nos aynkon**tra**mos]

When do we get back?
¿Cuándo regresamos? [**kwan**do raygray**sa**mos]

Do we have

¿Tenemos [tay**nay**mos]

time to ourselves?
algún tiempo libre? [al**goon** tee**aym**po **lee**bray]

time to go shopping?
tiempo para hacer compras? [tee**aym**po **pa**ra⌣a**thayr kom**pras]

Do we also visit...?
¿Visitamos también...? [veese**ta**mos tam**beeayn**]

Aiguablava Bay on the Costa Brava is just one of many popular haunts for amateur yachting enthusiasts

Active Pursuits

At the beach and at the swimming pool

Is there... around here?	¿Hay por aquí [aee por‿akee]
an open air/indoor swimming pool	una piscina/una piscina cubierta [oona peestheena/oona peestheena koobeeayrta]
a place to hire boats?	barcas para alquilar? [barkas para‿alkeelar]
Is it far to the beach?	¿Está lejos la playa? [aysta laykhos la playa]
When is low tide/high tide?	¿A qué hora tenemos marea baja/marea alta? [a kay‿ora taynaymos maraya bakha/maraya‿alta]
Is there a strong current?	¿La corriente es peligrosa? [la koreeayntay‿ays payleegrosa]
Are there jellyfish/sea urchins in the water?	¿Hay medusas/erizos de mar? [aee maydoosas/ayreethos day mar]

I'd like/We'd like to hire	Quería/Queríamos alquilar [kayreea/kayreeamos alkeelar]
a pedal/rowing boat	una barca de pedales/de remos [oona barka day paydalays/day raymos]
a motor/sailing boat	una lancha motora/un barco de vela [oona lancha motora/oon barko day bayla]
a deckchair	una tumbona [oona toombona]
a parasol	una sombrilla [oona sombreeya]
a surfboard	una tabla de surf [oona tabla day surf]
a pair of water skis	esquís náuticos [ayskees na-ooteekos]

How much is it	¿Cuánto cuesta [kwanto kwaysta]
per (half) hour	por (media) hora [por (maydeea) ora]
per day	por día [por deea]
per week?	por semana? [por saymana]

53

Danger signs

¡Aviso de tempestad!	Storm warning!
¡Peligro!	Danger!
¡Prohibido bañarse!	No swimming!
¡Prohibido saltar al agua!	No jumping!
¡Sólo para nadadores!	Swimmers only!

Are there... around here? ¿Hay por aquí [aee por_akee]
  sailing schools escuelas de navegación a vela
    [ayskooaylas day navaygatheeon a bayla]
  surfing schools escuelas de surf [ayskooaylas day surf]
  diving schools escuelas de buceo? [ayskooaylas day boothayo]
I'm a beginner/I'm experienced Soy principiante/avanzado (-a) [soy preentheepeeantay/abanthado (-a)]

Sports

Is there... around here? ¿Hay por aquí [aee por_akee]
  a (crazy) golf course un campo de (mini-)golf [oon kampo day (meenee-)golf]
  a tennis court una pista de tenis? [oona peesta day taynis]

Where can I ¿Dónde se puede [donday say pwayday]
  hire bicycles? alquilar bicicletas? [alkeelar beetheeklaytas]
  go bowling? jugar a los bolos? [khoogar a los bolos]
  go horse riding? montar a caballo? [montar a kaba-yo]
  play squash? jugar al squash? [khoogar al skooas]
  table tennis? jugar al ping-pong? [khoogar al ping pong]

Where can I take ¿Dónde puedo hacer aquí [donday pwaydo_athayr akee]
  tennis lessons un curso de tenis [oon koorso day taynis]
  skiing lessons un curso de esquí? [oon koorso day_ayskee]
Is fishing/swimming allowed here? ¿Aquí se puede pescar con caña/bañarse? [akee say pwayday payskar kon kanya/banyarsay]

I'd like/We'd like to hire Quería/Queríamos alquilar [kayreea/kayreeamos alkeelar]
  ice skating boots patines [pateenays]
  a tennis racket. una raqueta de tenis [oona rakayta day taynis]
I'd like a ski pass for one day/half a day/one week. Quería un pase para el telesquí para un día/medio día/una semana [kayreea_oon pasay para_ayl taylayskee para_oon deea/maydeeo deea/oona saymana]

Do you play chess? ¿Usted juega al ajedrez? [oostay khooayga_al akhaydrayth]

Do you mind if I join in? ¿Puedo jugar yo también? [pwaydo khoogar yo tambeeayn]

I'd like/We'd like to see	Quería/Queríamos ver [kayreea/kayreeamos bayr]
the football match	el partido de fútbol [ayl parteedo day footbol]
the competition	la competición [la kompayteetheeon]
the regatta	la regata [la raygata]
When does the match/the race start?	¿Cuándo comienza el juego/la carrera? [kwando komeeayntha ayl khooaygo/la karayra]
Where does it take place?	¿Dónde tiene lugar? [donday teeaynay loogar]

Active pursuits

arm bands	flotadores (m/pl) [flotadorays]
avalanche	avalancha [avalancha]
badminton	badmintón (m) [badmeenton]
ball	pelota; balón (large ball) (m) [paylota/balon]
bay	bahía [baeea]
basketball	baloncesto [balonthaysto]
billiards	billar (m) [beeyar]
changing rooms	caseta de baños [kasayta day banyos]
cross-country course	pista de fondo [peesta day fondo]
diving equipment	equipo de bucear [aykeepo day boothayar]
flippers	aletas [alaytas]
gymnastics	gimnasia [kheemnaseea]
health club	gimnasio [kheemnaseeo]
horse	caballo [kaba-yo]
jogging	footing (m) [footeeng]
playground	parque (m) infantil [parkay eenfanteel]
pony	poney (m) [pone-ee]
rubber dinghy	bote neumático (m) [botay nayoomateeko]
shade	sombra [sombra]
shells	concha [koncha]
sledge	trineo [treenayo]
snorkel	bucear con tubo respirador [boothayar kon toobo rayspeerador]
snow	nieve (f) [neeaybay]
sport	deporte (m) [dayportay]
stadium	estadio [aystadeeo]
storm	tempestad (f) [taympaysta]
suntan lotion	crema solar [krayma solar]
volleyball	balónvolea (m) [balonbolaya]
water temperature	temperatura del agua [taympayratoora dayl agooa]
wave	ola [ola]

55

Nature, environment, adventure

We'd like	**Queríamos** [kay**ree**amos]
to go on a bicycle tour	hacer excursiones en bicicleta [a**thayr** ayxkoor**seeon**ays ayn beethee**klay**ta]
to go hiking	hacer una excursión por la montaña [a**thayr oo**na ayxkoor**seeon** por la mon**ta**nya]
to go trekking	hacer excursiones a pie [a**thayr** ayxkoor**seeo**nays a peeay]
Do you have	**¿Tiene *(sing)*/Tienen *(pl)*** [**teeay**nay/ **teeay**nayn]
a hiking map?	un mapa de excursiones [oon **ma**pa day‿eyxkoor**seeo**nays]
a map of cycle paths?	un mapa de excursiones en bicicleta? [oon **ma**pa day‿ayxkoor**seeo**nays en beethee**klay**ta]
Are there any suggestions for hiking in this region?	¿Hay itinerarios elaborados para esta región? [aee‿eeteenay**ra**reeos aylabo**ra**dos **para‿ay**sta re**kheeon**]
Is the route	**¿El itinerario está** [ayl eeteenay**ra**reeo‿ay**sta**]
well marked	bien señalado [beeayn sayn-ya**la**do]
suitable for children?	apto para niños? [**ap**to **pa**ra **nee**nyos]
How many kilometres is it?/ How many hours does it take?	¿Cuántos kilómetros/Cuántas horas son? [**kwan**tos kee**lo**maytros/**kwan**tas **o**ras son]
Where can I find a mountain guide?	¿Dónde encuentro un guía de montaña? [**don**day‿ayn**kooayn**tro‿oon **gee**a day mon**ta**nya]
Is this the right way to...?	¿Es el camino para...? [ays ayl ka**mee**no **pa**ra]
How far is it to...?	¿Falta mucho para...? [**fa**lta **moo**cho **pa**ra]

Courses

I'd like to attend	**Quería inscribirme a** [kay**ree**a eenskree**beer**may‿a]
a language course/Spanish course	un curso de lenguas/de español [oon **koor**so day **layn**gooas/day‿ayspa**nyol**]
a cookery/painting course	un curso de cocina/de pintura [oon **koor**so day ko**thee**na/day peen**too**ra]
a (theatre/dance) workshop.	un seminario (de teatro/de baile) [oon saymee**na**reeo (day tay**a**tro/day **baee**lay)]
Are there still places available?	¿Hay todavía plazas libres? [aee toda**vee**a **pla**thas **lee**brays]
Where does the course take place?	¿Dónde tiene lugar el curso? [**don**day **teeay**nay loo**gar** el **koor**so]
How many people are taking part in the course?	¿Cuántos participantes hay en el curso? [**kwan**tos parteethee**pan**tays aee‿ayn ayl **koor**so]
When does it start?/How much is the course?	¿Cuándo empieza/Cuánto cuesta el curso? [**kwan**do‿aym**peeay**tha/**kwan**to **kway**sta‿ayl **koor**so]
Do you have somebody to look after the children?	¿Hay guardería para los niños? [aee gooarday**ree**a **pa**ra los **nee**nyos]

The pilgrimage to the Virgen del Rocío in Huelva province, the largest in Spain, is a good excuse for a lively fiesta

Entertainment

Cinema, theatre, opera and concerts

What's on at the cinema today/tomorrow?

¿Qué películas ponen hoy/ mañana en el cine? [kay pay**lee**koolas **po**nayn oee/man**ya**na‿ayn ayl **thee**nay]

Is the film
dubbed?
shown in the original version with subtitles?

¿La película está [la pe**lee**koola‿ay**sta**]
doblada? [do**bla**da]
en voz original con subtítulos?
[ayn both oreekhee**nal** kon soob**tee**toolos]

When does... start?

¿A qué hora empieza
[a kay‿ora‿aympee**ay**tha]

the show
the film
the concert
the matinée

la sesión? [la say**seeon**]
la película? [la pay**lee**koola]
el concierto? [ayl kon**thee**ayrto]
la función matinal?
[la foon**theeon** matee**nal**]

the recital
the ballet performance
the cabaret
the opera
the operetta
the musical
the play
the ticket sale

el recital [ayl raythee**tal**]]
el ballet? [ayl ba-**yay**]
el cabaré? [ayl kaba**ray**]
la ópera? [la‿**o**payra]
la opereta? [la‿opay**ray**ta]
el musical? [ayl moosee**kal**]
el teatro? [ayl tay**a**tro]
la venta anticipada de entradas?
[la **bayn**ta‿anteethee**epa**da day ayn**tra**das]

for the (music) festival?

para el festival (de música)?
[**pa**ra‿ayl faystee**val** (day **moo**seeka)]

57

At the theatre

Anfiteatro	upper circle	**Izquierda**	left
Anfiteatro/Galería	circle	**Lateral**	aisle
Asiento/Localidad	seat	**Lavabos**	toilets
Centro	centre	**Palco**	box
Derecha	right	**Piso principal**	dress circle
Entrada	entrance	**Platea**	stalls
Fila	row	**Salida**	exit

What's on
tonight/tomorrow night?

this weekend?

at the theatre?
at the opera?
Where do I get/How much are
the tickets?

Are there still tickets at the
box office?
Are there special rates?

* ¡Agotado! [agotado]

¿Qué ponen [kay ponayn]
hoy/mañana por la noche?
[oy/manyana por la nochay]
este fin de semana? [aystay feen day
saymana]
en el teatro? [ayn ayl tayatro]
en la ópera? [ayn la‿opayra]
¿Dónde se venden/Cuánto cuestan las
entradas? [donday say vayndayn/kwanto
kwaystan las ayntradas]
¿Quedan entradas en la taquilla?
[kaydan ayntradas ayn la takeeya]
¿Hay entradas a precio reducido?
[aee ayntradas a praytheeo raydootheedo]
Sold out!

Two tickets/seats..., please

for the show
for the concert
tonight/tomorrow night

at 8 o'clock
How long does the show last?

I would like a programme,
please

Dos entradas por favor [dos ayntradas por
favor]
para la sesión [para la sayseeon]
para el concierto [para‿ayl kontheeayrto]
de hoy/mañana por la noche
[day‿oee/manyana por la nochay]
a las veinte horas [a las vay-eentay‿oras]
¿Cuánto tiempo dura la función?
[kwanto teeaympo doora la foontheeon]
¿Me da un programa, por favor?
[may dah‿oon programa por favor]

Nightlife

Is there... around here?
a disco
a pub
a bar
a casino
with live music?

Is this seat taken?

Could I see the wine list,
please

¿Hay por aquí [aee por‿akee]
una discoteca [oona deeskotayka]
una tasca [oona taska]
un club nocturno [oon kloob noktoorno]
un casino [oon kaseeno]
con música en directo?
[kon mooseeka‿ayn deeraykto]
¿Este asiento está libre?
[aystay‿aseeaynto‿aysta leebray]
La carta de vinos, por favor
[la karta day beenos por favor]

Entertainment

actor	actor [ak**tor**]
actress	actriz [ak**treeth**]
applaud	aplaudir [aplaoo**deer**]; *(rhythmic)* dar palmadas [dar pal**ma**das]
ballet	ballet [ba-**yay**]
band	banda/conjunto [**ban**da/kon**khoon**to]
bar	club nocturno *(m)* [kloob nok**toor**no]
box office	caja [**ka**kha]
cabaret	cabaret *(m)* [kaba**ray**]
chamber music	música de cámara [**moo**seeka day **ka**mara]
choir	coro [**ko**ro]
circus	circo [**theer**ko]
comedy	comedia [ko**may**deea]
conductor	director *(m)* de orquesta [deerayk**tor** day_or**kay**sta]
curtain	telón [tay**lon**]
dance	bailar [baee**lar**]
dancer	bailarín *(m)* [baeela**reen**]
	bailarina *(f)* [baeela**ree**na]
director	director(a) de cine [deerayk**tor**(a) day **thee**nay]
dressing room	guardarropa [gooarda**ro**pa]
exit	salir [sa**leer**]
Flamenco	baile de flamenco *(m)* [**baee**lay day fla**mayn**ko]
interval	descanso [days**kan**so]
jazz concert	concierto de jazz [konthee**ayr**to day chas]
More!	¡Otra! [**otra**]
open-air cinema/theatre	cine *(m)*/teatro al aire libre [**thee**nay/tay**a**tro al_**aee**ray **lee**bray]
opera glasses	gemelos *(m/pl)* [khay**may**los]
orchestra	orquesta [or**kay**sta]
play	jugar [khoo**gar**]; *(Instrument)* tocar [to**kar**]
pop music	música pop [**moo**seeka pop]
première	estreno [ay**stray**no]
presentation/show	representación *(f)* [ray-pray-saynt-athee**on**]
programme	programa [pro**gra**ma]
singer	cantante *(m/f)* [kan**tan**tay]
Spanish operetta	zarzuela [thartho**oay**la]
stage	escena [ay**sthay**na]
stage set	escenografía [aysthaynogra**fee**a]
ticket	entrada [ayn**tra**da]
ticket sale	venta anticipada [**bayn**ta_antee**thee**pada]
usher	acomodador [akomoda**dor**]

Shall we	¿Le gustaría [lay goostareea]
dance?	bailar? [baeelar]
have a drink?	tomar algo? [tomar⌣algo]
get a bit of fresh air?	tomar el aire? [tomar ayl⌣aeeray]
go for a stroll?	dar una vuelta? [dar⌣oona vwaylta]

This one's on me.	Le invito [lay⌣eenbeeto]

Can I	¿Me permite acompañarla [may payrmeetay⌣akompanyarla]
walk with you for a while?	un rato [oon rato]
walk you home?	a casa [a kasa]
walk you to the hotel?	al hotel? [al⌣otayl]
Would you like to come to my place?	¿Vamos a mi casa? [bamos a mee kasa]
Thank you very much for the nice evening.	Muchas gracias por esta noche tan bella. [moochas gratheeas por⌣aysta nochay tan bay-a]
Goodbye./See you tomorrow!	Adiós/Hasta mañana [adeeos/asta manyana]

Festivals and events

When does... start?	¿Cuándo empieza [kwando⌣aympeeaytha]
the festival	la fiesta? [la feeaysta]
the festival programme	el programa festivo? [ayl programa faysteevo]
the Mass	la misa? [la meesa]
the fair	la feria? [la fayreea])
the parade/procession	el desfile/la procesión [ayl daysfeelay/la prothayseeon]
the show/performance	el espectáculo [ayl ayspayktakoolo]
the circus?	el circo? [ayl theerko]
Where does the show take place?	¿Dónde tiene lugar la representación? [donday teeaynay loogar la raypraysayntatheeon]
How long will it last?	¿Cuánto tiempo durará? [kwanto teeaympo doorara]
Do you have to pay an entrance charge?	¿Hay que pagar por la entrada? [aee kay pagar por la ayntrada]
How much are the tickets?	¿Cuánto cuestan las entradas? [kwanto kwaystan las ayntradas]

Christmas and New Year

"Happy Christmas" in Spanish is ¡Feliz Navidad! [fayleeth naveeda]. Spanish children do not receive their presents on Christmas Day; they must wait until the evening of the 5th January. This is when the Reyes Magos [ray-ees makhos], the Three Kings, arrive by sea laden with parcels.

On New Year's Eve, called Noche Vieja [nochay beeaykha], practically every Spaniard follows the 12 strokes of a famous Madrid clock live on TV or radio, swallowing one "lucky" grape or uvas de la suerte [oobas day la swayrtay] for each stroke. This is to encourage good luck in the year ahead,

Shops in Spain stay open until late in the evening, but they often close for the afternoon, usually from 1 to 5pm

Shopping

General

Where can I get	**¿Dónde puedo comprar** [donday **pway**do kom**prar**]
films/newspapers?	carretes/periódicos? [ka**ray**tays/pay**reeo**deekos]
Is there... around here?	**¿Hay por aquí** [aee por‿a**kee**]
a bakery	una panadería [oona panaday**ree**a]
a food store	una tienda de comestibles [**oo**na tee**ayn**da day komay**stee**blays]
a butcher's shop	una carnicería [**oo**na karneethay**ree**a]
a supermarket	un supermercado? [oon soopayrmayr**ka**do]
* ¿Qué desea? [kay‿day**say**-a]	What would you like?
* ¿Puedo ayudarle? [**pway**do‿ayoo**dar**lay]	Can I help you?
I'm just looking, thanks	Quería sólo mirar [kay**ree**a **so**lo mee**rar**]
I'd like..., please	**Quisiera..., por favor** [kee**seeay**ra... por fa**vor**]
stamps	sellos [**say**os]
suntan lotion	una crema solar [**oo**na **kray**ma so**lar**]
How much is this?	¿Cuánto cuesta? [**kwan**to **kway**sta]
That's (too) expensive	Es (demasiado) caro [ays (dayma**seea**do) **ka**ro]
I (don't) like that	Eso (no) me gusta [**ay**so (no) may **goo**sta]
I'll take it	Me lo quedo [may lo **kay**do]
Do you have anything cheaper/larger/smaller?	¿Tiene algo más barato/más grande/más pequeño? [tee**ay**nay‿**al**go mas ba**ra**to/mas **gran**day/mas pay**kay**nyo]

61

Groceries

baby food	alimento para bebés [alee**mayn**to **para** bay**bays**]
biscuits	galletas [ga**yay**tas]
cake	pastel *(m)* [pas**tayl**]
chocolate (bar)	(barrita de) chocolate *(m)* [(ba**ree**ta day) choko**la**tay]
cocoa	cacao [ka**kao**]
(without) colouring	(sin) colorantes [(seen) kolo**ran**tays]
cream	nata [**na**ta]
eggs	huevos [**ooay**bos]
fish	pescado [pay**ska**do]
flour	harina [a**ree**na]
fruit	fruta [**froo**ta]
juice	zumo [**thoo**mo]
ketchup	ketchup *(m)* [**kay**choop]
margarine	margarina [marga**ree**na]
mayonnaise	mayonesa [ma-eeo**nay**sa]
meat	carne *(f)* [**kar**nay]
(full-cream/semi-skimmed) milk	leche *(f)* (entera/semidesnatada) [**lay**chay (ayn**tay**ra/saymeedaysna**ta**da)]
mustard	mostaza [mo**sta**tha]
nuts	nueces *(f/Pl)* [**nooay**thays]
oil	aceite *(m)* [a**thay-ee**tay]
paprika	pimentón *(m)* [peemayn**ton**]
pepper	pimienta [peem**eeayn**ta]
porridge oats	copos de havena [**ko**pos day ̲a**bay**na]
(without) preservatives	(sin) conservantes *(m/pl)* [(seen) konsayr**ban**tays]
sponge cake/finger	bizcocho [beeth**ko**cho]
salt	sal *(f)* [sal]
sausage	salchicha [sal**chee**cha]
spices	especias *(f/pl)* [ay**spay**theeas]
sugar	azúcar *(m)* [a**thoo**kar]
tinned foods	conservas [kon**sayr**bas]
toast	tostada [to**sta**da]
vegetables	verduras [bayr**doo**ras]
vinegar	vinagre *(m)* [beena**gray**]

▶ (*See also* **food**, *page* 44)

Fruit and vegetables

apple	manzana [man**tha**na]
apricot	albaricoque *(m)* [albaree**ko**kay]
artichoke	alcachofa [alka**cho**fa]
aubergine	berenjena [bayrayn**khay**na]
avocado	aguacate [agooa**ka**tay]

banana	plátano [**pla**tano]
basil	basilico [ba**see**leeko]
beans (runner/haricot)	judías (verdes/blancas) [khoo**dee**as (**bayr**days/**blan**kas)]
broccoli	brócoli *(m)* [**bro**kolee]
cabbage	col *(m)* [kol]
carrots	zanahorias [thana**o**reeas]
celery	apio [**a**peeo]
cherries	cerezas [thay**ray**thas]
chicory	endibia [aynd**ee**beea]
corn	maíz [ma**eeth**]
courgette	calabacín *(m)* [kalaba**theen**]
cucumber	pepino [pay**pee**no]
dates	dátiles *(m)* [**da**teelays]
figs	higos [**ee**gos]
garlic	ajo [**a**kho]
grapefruit	pomelo [po**may**lo]
grapes (white/red)	uvas (blancas/negras) [**oo**bas (**blan**kas/**nay**gras)]
kiwi	kiwi *(m)* [**kee**wee]
leek	puerro [**pway**ro]
lemon	limón *(m)* [lee**mon**]
lettuce	lechuga [lay**choo**ga]
mandarin orange	mandarina [manda**ree**na]
mango	mango [**man**go]
melon (honeydew)	melón *(m)* [may**lon**]
mushrooms	champiñones/setas [champeen**yon**ays/**say**tas]
olives	aceitunas [athayee**too**nas]
onion	cebolla [thay**bo**ya]
orange	naranja [na**ran**kha]
parsley	perejil *(m)* [payray**kheel**]
peach	melocotón *(m)* [mayloko**ton**]
peanuts	cacahuetes *(m)* [kaka**ooay**tays]
pear	pera [**pay**ra]
peas	guisantes *(m)* [gee**san**tays]
pineapple	piña [**pee**nya]
plum	ciruela [thee**roo**ayla]
potatoes	patatas [pa**ta**tas]
raspberries	frambuesas [fram**booay**sas]
spinach	espinacas *(f/pl)* [ayspee**na**kas]
strawberries	fresas [**fray**sas]
sweet pepper	pimiento [peemee**aynt**o]
tomato	tomate *(m)* [to**ma**tay]
turnip	nabo [**na**bo]
water melon	sandía [san**dee**a]

Can I

pay by cheque/credit card

exchange this?
Where's the nearest
cash dispenser/
the nearest bank?

¿Puedo [pwaydo]

pagar con cheque/tarjeta de crédito
[pagar kon chaykay/tarkhayta day kraydeeto]
cambiar eso? [kambeear_ayso]
¿Dónde está el cajero automático/
el banco más cercano?
[donday_aysta ayl kakhayro_aootomateeko/
ayl banko mas thayrkano]

* ¿Algo más? [algo mas]
That's all, thanks
Could you pack it for me,
please?
Do you have a carrier bag?

Anything else?
No gracias, es todo [no gratheeas ays todo]
¿Me lo puede empaquetar?
[may lo pwayday_aympakaytar]
¿Me da una bolsa? [may da_oona bolsa]

Groceries

**I'd like/Could I have...,
please?**

a piece of...
100 grams of...
half a kilo/a kilo of...

a litre of...
a tin/bottle of...

Could I try some of this,
please?
* Es un poco más, ¿vale?
[es oon poko mas valay]
A bit more/less, please

It's all right!

Quería/Deme..., por favor
[kayreea/daymay... por favor]

una pieza de... [oona peeaytha day]
cien gramos de... [theeayn gramos day]
medio kilo/un kilo de...
[maydeeo keelo/oon keelo day]
un litro de... [oon leetro day]
una lata/botella de... [oona lata/botaya
day]
¿Puedo probar? [pwaydo probar]

It's a bit over. Is that all right?

Un poco más/menos, por favor
[oon poko mas/maynos por favor]
Está bien así [esta bee-ayn_asee]

Books, stationery and newspapers

Do you sell

English papers/magazines

postcards
stamps
writing paper
envelopes
pens
pencils
English books

glue/adhesive tape?

¿Tienen [teeaynayn]

periódicos/revistas ingleses?
[payreeodeekos /raybeestas eenglaysays]
postales? [postales]
sellos? [sayos]
papel de cartas? [papayl day kartas]
sobres? [sobrays]
bolígrafos? [boleegrafos]
lápices? [lapeethays]
libros ingleses?
[leebros eenglaysays]
pegamento/cinta adhesiva?
[paygamaynto/theenta_adayseeba]

I'd like

a map of...
a street map

Quería [kayreea]

un mapa de... [oon mapa day]
un plano de la ciudad
[oon plano day la theeooda]

a hiking map	un mapa de excursiones [oon **ma**pa day ayxkoor**see**onays]
a Spanish–English dictionary	un diccionario español-ingles [oon deektheeona**ree**o⌣ayspa**nyol** een**glay**s]

Clothes and shoes

I'm looking for	Estoy buscando [e**stoy** boos**kan**do]
a blouse/a shirt	una blusa/una camisa [**oo**na **bloo**sa/**oo**na ka**mee**sa]
a T-shirt	una camiseta [**oo**na kamee**say**ta]
a pair of trousers/a skirt/ a dress	unos pantalones/una falda/ un vestido [**oo**nos panta**lo**nays/**oo**na **fal**da/ oon bay**stee**do]
a sweater/a jacket	un jersey/una chaqueta [oon khayr**say**/**oo**na cha**kay**ta]
underwear/socks	ropa interior/calcetines [**ro**pa⌣eenta**yree**or/kalthay**tee**nays]
a raincoat	un impermeable [oon eempayrmaye**ab**lay]
a pair of shoes for ladies/men/ children.	zapatos [tha**pa**tos] para señoras/señores/niños. [**pa**ra sayn-**yor**as/sayn-**yor**ays/**neen**yos]
I want size 40	Necesito la talla cuarenta [naythay**see**to la **ta**ya kwa**rayn**ta] .
I take size 39	Calzo el número treinta y nueve [**kal**tho ayl **noo**mayro **tray**-eenta⌣ee **noo**ay**bay**]
Could I try this on?	¿Puedo probármelo? [**pway**do pro**bar**maylo]
Do you have a mirror?	¿Dónde hay un espejo? [**don**day⌣aee⌣oon ay**spay**kho]
It fits (doesn't fit) well	(No) Queda bien [(no) **kay**da bee-**ayn**]
I like/I don't like it/this colour	Esto/Este color (no) me gusta [**ay**sto/**ay**stay ko**lor** (no) may **goo**sta]
I'll take it	Me lo llevo [may lo **yev**o]
Do you have other styles/ colours?	¿Hay otros modelos/otros colores? [aee⌣**o**tros mo**day**los/**o**tros ko**lor**ays]

It is	**Es** [es]
too small/big	demasiado pequeño/grande [dayma**see**ado⌣pay**kay**nyo/**gran**day]
too long/short	desmasiado largo/corto [dayma**see**ado **lar**go/**kor**to]
too tight/loose	demasiado estrecho/ancho [dayma**see**ado ay**stray**cho/**an**cho]

Is this	**¿Es** [es]
real leather	cuero [**kway**ro]
cotton/wool/silk/linen?	algodón/lana/seda/lino? [algo**don**/**la**na/**say**da/**lee**no]

Clothes and shoes

anorak	anorak *(m)* [**an**orak]
belt	cinturón *(m)* [theentoo**ron**]
bikini	bikini *(m)* [bee**kee**nee]
boots	botas [**bo**tas]
bra	sostén *(m)* [sos**tayn**]
cap	gorra [**go**ra]
cardigan	rebeca [re**bek**ah]
gloves	guantes *(m/pl)* [**gwan**tays]
hat (straw)	sombrero (de paja) [som**bray**ro (day **pa**kha)]
jeans	tejanos [tay**kha**nos]
knee socks	mini-medias [meenee **may**deeas]
knickers	bragas [**bra**gas]
pyjamas	pijama *(m)* [pee**kha**ma]
sandals	sandalias [san**da**leeas]
slippers	zapatillas *(f)* [thapa**tee**yas]
swimsuit	traje *(m)* de baño [**tra**khay day **ban**yo]
tie	corbata [kor**ba**ta]
tights	medias [**may**deeas]
tracksuit	chándal *(m)* [**chan**dal]
trunks	bañador *(m)* [banya**dor**]
underpants	calzoncillos [kalthon**thee**yos]
waistcoat	chaleco [cha**lay**ko]

Laundry and dry cleaning

I'd like to have these things washed/cleaned	Quiero que me lo laven/laven en seco [**keeay**ro kay may lo **la**vayn/**la**vayn en **say**ko]
How much is it?	¿Cuánto cuesta? [**kwan**to **kway**sta]
When will it be ready?	¿Cuándo estará listo? [**kwan**do⌣aysta**ra lee**sto]

Jewellery and watches

My necklace/my watch/ my alarm clock is broken	Mi collar/Mi reloj/Mi despertador está estropeado [mee ko**yar**/mee ray**lokh**/mee dayspayrta**dor** esta aystropa**ya**do]
Could you repair it?	¿Me lo puede arreglar? [may lo **pway**day⌣array**glar**]

I'd like	**Quisiera** [kee**seeay**ra]
a new battery	una nueva pila [**oo**na **noo**ayba **pee**la]
a bracelet	una pulsera [**oo**na pool**say**ra]
a brooch	un broche [oon **bro**chay]
a ring	un anillo [oon a**nee**yo]
some earrings	unos pendientes [**o**nos payndee**ayn**tays]

Is this	¿Es [ays]
genuine	auténtico [aootaynteeko]
silver/gold	de plata/de oro [day **pla**ta/day‿oro]
silver-plated/gold-plated?	plateado/dorado? [plata**ya**do/do**ra**do]

Electrical appliances and photography

I'm looking for/I need
Estoy buscando/Necesito
[es**too**ee boos**kan**do/naythay**see**to]

an adapter — un adaptador [oon adapta**dor**]
a battery — una pila [**oo**na **pee**la]
  for a walkman — para el walkman [para ayl **wal**man]
  for a torch — para la linterna [para la leen**tayr**na]
  for a camera — para la cámara fotográfica
    [para la **ka**mara fotogra**fee**ka]
  for a video camera — para la cámara de vídeo
    [para la **ka**mara de **bee**dayo]
  for a radio — para la radio [para la **ra**deeo]

I'd like
Quisiera [kee**see**ayra]
a colour film — un carrete en color
  [oon ka**ray**tay‿ayn ko**lor**]
a black and white film — un carrete en blanco y negro
  [oon ka**ray**tay‿ayn **blan**ko‿ee **nay**gro]
a slide film — un carrete de diapositivas
  [oon ka**ray**tay day deeapo**see**teebas]
  with 24 (36) exposures — de veinticuatro (treinta y seis) fotos
    [day bay-eentee**kwa**tro
    (tray-**een**ta‿ee say-**ees**) **fo**tos]
a video cassette — una videocasete [**oo**na beedayoka**say**tay]
a standard lens — un objetivo estándar
  [oon obkhay**tee**bo‿ay**stan**dar]
a telephoto lens — un teleobjetivo [oon taylayobkhay**tee**bo]

Could you..., please?
¿Me puede [may **pway**day]
  put the film in the camera — poner el carrete [po**nayr** ayl ka**ray**tay]
  develop this film for me — revelar este carrete [rayvay**lar** ay**stay** ka**ray**tay]
  make copies — hacer copias [a**thayr** ko**pee**as]
    9 by 13 — nueve por trece [noo**oo**aybay por **tray**thay]
    gloss/matt — brillante/mate? [bree**yan**tay/**ma**tay]
Do you do passport photos? — ¿Aquí se hacen fotos de pasaporte?
  [a**kee** say‿a**thayn** fotos day pasa**por**tay]

When will the prints be ready? — ¿Cuándo estarán listas?
  [**kwan**do‿ay**sta**ran **lee**stas]

...doesn't work
...no funciona bien [no foonthee**o**na bee-ayn]
  My camera — Mi cámara [mee **ka**mara]
  My flash — El flash [ayl flasch]
  My video camera — Mi cámara de vídeo [mee **ka**mara day **bee**dayo]
Could you have a look at it?/ — ¿Puede revisarlo/arreglarlo?
  Can you repair it? — [**pway**day rayvee**sar**lo/aray**glar**lo]
When can I pick it up? — ¿Cuándo puedo recogerlo?
  [**kwan**do **pway**do rayko**khayr**lo]

Souvenirs and art and crafts

I'm looking for	Estoy buscando [estoy booskando]
a souvenir	un recuerdo [oon raykooayrdo]
folk costumes	trajes tradicionales [trakhays tradeetheeonalays]
ceramics	cerámica [thayrameeka]
art	objetos de arte [obkhaytos day‿artay]
modern	modernos [modayrnos]
antique	antiguos [anteegoo-os]
folk	populares [popoolarays]
leather goods	artículos de piel [arteekoolos day peeayl]
jewellery	joyas [khoyas]

What's typical of	¿Cuáles son las cosas típicas de [kwalays son las kosas teepeekas day)
this town?	esta ciudad? [aysta theeoodad]
this area?	esta región? [aysta raykheeon]
this country?	este país? [ayste pa-ees]

Is this	¿Es [es]
genuine/antique?	auténtico/antiguo? [aootaynteeko/anteegwo]
artisan work?	artesanía? [artaysaneea]
local?	de aquí? [day‿akee]
Is this handmade?	¿Está hecho a mano? [aysta‿aycho‿a mano]

Optician

My glasses are broken	Mis gafas están rotas [mees gafas aystan rotas]
Can you repair them/ let me have a spare pair?	¿Puede arreglármelas/darme unas gafas de repuesto? [pwayday arayglarmaylas/ darmay‿oonas gafas day raypwaysto]
When will the glasses be ready?	¿Cuándo estarán listas las gafas? [kwando‿aystaran leestas las gafas]

Tobacco and more

Spanish tobacconists or *estancos* sell cigarettes (*cigarrillos*), cigars (*puros*) and cigarillos (*puritos*). But these little shops, easily identified by the brown and gold sign spelling out *Tabacos* also sell a range of important everyday items, such as phone cards (*tarjetas telefónicas*), stamps (*sellos*), postcards (*postales*), envelopes (*sobres*) and other writing materials, although they do not stock newspapers (*periódicos*) and magazines (*revistas*).

I have lost my glasses/one of my contact lenses	He perdido mis gafas/una lentilla [ay payr**dee**do mees **ga**fas/**oo**na layn**tee**ya]
I'm shortsighted/longsighted	Soy miope/présbita [soy mee**o**pay/**prays**beeta]
I have… dioptres in the right/left eye	Tengo… dioptrías en el ojo derecho/ en el ojo izquierdo [**tayn**go deeop**tree**as ayn ayl **o**kho day**ray**cho/ ayn ayl **o**kho eethkee**ayr**do]

I need	**Necesito** [naythay**see**to]
a pair of sunglasses	unas gafas de sol [**oo**nas **ga**fas day sol]
a spectacle case	un estuche para las gafas [oon ays**too**chay **pa**ra las **ga**fas]
a pair of binoculars	unos prismáticos [**oo**nos prees**ma**teekos]
cleansing solution	un líquido para limpiar [on **lee**keedo **pa**ra leem**pee**ar]
rinsing solution	un líquido para conservar [oon **lee**keedo **pa**ra konsayr**var**]
for hard/soft contact lenses	para lentillas duras/blandas [**pa**ra layn**tee**yas **doo**ras/**blan**das]

Chemist

I'd like	**Quería** [kay**ree**a]
some plasters	un esparadrapo [oon ayspara**dra**po]
some tissues	pañuelos de papel [pan**yoo**ay**los** day pa**payl**]
a hand/skin cream	una crema para las manos/para la piel [**oo**na **kray**ma **pa**ra las **ma**nos/ **pa**ra la pee**ayl**]
a suntan lotion	una crema solar [**oo**na **kray**ma so**lar**]
with protection factor 12	con factor de protección solar doce [kon fak**tor** day protaykthee**on** so**lar do**thay]
a lipstick	un pintalabios [peenta**la**beeos]
a shampoo	un champú [oon cham**poo**]
for normal/dry/greasy hair	para pelo normal/seco/graso [**pa**ra **pay**lo nor**mal**/**say**ko/**gra**so]
for dandruff	contra la caspa [**kon**tra la **kas**pa]
a baby's bottle	un biberón [oon beebay**ron**]
a dummy	un chupete [oon choo**pay**tay]
nappies	pañales [pan**ya**lays]
baby powder	polvos de talco [**pol**bos day **tal**ko]
something for a headache	algo para un dolor de cabeza [**al**go para oon do**lor** day ca**bay**tha]

Tobacconist

..., please
  A packet/carton of
  cigarettes

    with/without filters
  A packet of pipe tobacco
  A box of matches
  A lighter

Por favor, deme [por fa**vor day**may]
  un paquete/un cartón de cigarrillos
  [oon pa**kay**tay/oon kar**ton** day
  theega**ree**yos]
    con/sin filtro [kon/seen **feel**tro]
  tabaco de pipa [ta**ba**ko day **pee**pa]
  cerillas [thay**ree**yas]
  un encendedor [oon aynthaynday**dor**]

Chemist

after-shave	loción *(f)* de afeitar [lo**theeon** day⌣afay-ee**tar**]
baby's bottle	biberón *(m)* [beebay**ron**]
brush	cepillo [thay**peel**yo]
comb	peine *(m)* [**pay-ee**nay]
condom	condón *(m)* [kon**don**]/ preservativo [praysayrba**tee**bo]
cotton wool	algodón *(m)* [algo**don**]
deodorant	desodorante *(m)* [daysodo**ran**tay]
dummy	chupete *(m)* [choo**pay**tay]
hairspray	laca/spray *(m)* [**la**ka/**spraee**]
insect repellent	repelente *(m)* [raypay**layn**tay]
mirror	espejo [ay**spay**kho]
nail file	lima de uñas [**leema** day⌣**oo**nyas]
nail scissors	tijeras para las uñas [tee**khay**ras **para** las **oo**nyas]
nappies	pañales *(m)* [pan**ya**lays]
plaster	un esparadrapo [oon espara**dra**po]
razor-blade	hoja de afeitar [**okha** day⌣afay-ee**tar**]
saftey pin	imperdible *(m)* [eempayr**dee**blay]
sanitary towels	vendas (compresas higiénicas) [**bayn**das (kom**pray**sas eekhee**ayn**eekas]
shampoo	champú [cham**poo**]
shaving cream/foam	crema/espuma de afeitar [**kray**ma/ay**spoo**ma day⌣afay-ee**tar**]
shower gel	gel *(m)* para ducharse [khayl **para** doo**char**say]
soap	jabón *(m)* [kha**bon**]
tampons	tampones *(m)* [tam**po**nays]
toilet paper	papel *(m)* higiénico [pa**payl** eekhee**ayn**eeko]
toothbrush	cepillo [thay**pee**yo]
toothpaste	pasta de dientes [**pas**ta day **dee**ayntays]
tweezers	pinzas [**peen**thas]
washing-up liquid	lavavajillas *(m)* [lavava**khee**yas]
washing powder	detergente *(m)* [daytayr**khen**tay]

Practical Information

Medical assistance

At the doctor's surgery

I need a doctor (urgently)

Necesito un médico (urgentemente)
[nay thay**seeto**‿oon **may**deeko
(oor**khayn**taymayntay]

Please call a doctor/an
ambulance

Llame a un médico de urgencia/a una
ambulancia, por favor
[**ya**may a oon **may**deeko day‿oor**khayn**theea/
a‿**oo**na amboo**lan**theea por fa**vor**]

Is there a... around here?
 a doctor
 gynaecologist
 paediatrician
 dentist
  English-speaking
Can the doctor come here?

When is his surgery open?

Can I have an appointment
 immediately/wait here?
When can I come?
* ¿Qué le pasa? [kay‿lay **pa**sa]
I feel sick/faint

I had a fall
I've vomited

¿Hay por aquí [aee por‿a**kee**]
 un médico [oon **may**deeko]
 un ginecólogo [oon kheenay**ko**logo]
 un pediatra [oon payde**ea**tra]
 un dentista [oon dayn**tee**sta]
  que hable inglés [kay‿**a**blay‿een**glays**]
¿Puede venir el médico?
[**pway**day bay**neer** ayl **may**deeko]
¿A qué hora tiene consulta?
[a kay‿**ora tee**eaynay kon**sool**ta]
¿Puedo ir ahora/quedarme?
[**pway**do eer a-**o**ra/kay**dar**may]
¿Cuándo puedo ir? [**kwan**do **pway**do eer]
What can I do for you?
Me siento mal/me mareo
[may **seeayn**to mal/may ma**ray**o]
Me he caído [may‿**ay** ka**ee**do]
He vomitado [ay vome**ta**do]

72

I've got	Tengo [tayngo]
a cold	un resfriado [oon rayfreeado]
an allergy	una alergia [oona_alayrkheea]
diarrhoea	una diarrea [oona deearaya]
the flu/a cough	gripe/tos [greepay/tos]
a headache	dolor de cabeza [dolor day kabaytha]
stomach-ache	dolor de barriga [dolor day bareega]
earache	dolor de oído [dolor day_o-eedo]
a sore throat	dolor de garganta [dolor day gargantay]
cystitis	una cistitis [oona ceesteetees]
heart trouble	trastornos cardíacos
	[trastornos kardeeakos]
a (high) temperature.	(mucha) fiebre [(moocha) feeaybray]

* ¿Desde cuándo tiene fiebre?   When did the fever start?
[daysday kwando teeaynay
feeaybray]

Two days ago   Desde hace dos días
                               [daysday_athay dos deeas]

* ¿Dónde le duele?   Where does it hurt?
[donday lay dwaylay]

* No es nada grave   It's nothing serious
[no_ays nada gravay]

Is the arm/   ¿El brazo/El dedo está fracturado?
  the finger broken?   [ayl bratho/ayl daydo aysta fraktoorado]

I think the leg is broken   Creo que la pierna está fracturada
                               [krayo kay la peeayrna_aysta fraktoorada]

I've got digestion problems   No aguanto la comida [no agwanto la
                               komeeda]

I'm allergic to penicillin   No aguanto la penicilina [no agwanto la
                               peneetheeleena]

I'm (4 months) pregnant   Estoy embarazada (de cuatro meses)
                               [aystoy_aymbarathada
                               (day kwatro maysays]

I'm taking medication   Tomo medicamentos regularmente
                               [tomo maydeekamayntos raygoolarmayntay]

Could you	¿Me puede [may pwayday]
prescribe this for me	recetar eso [raythaytar ayso]
prescribe something for...,	recetar algo contra...?
please?	[raycaytar algo kontra]

Directions for use of medicine

antes/después de las comidas	before/after food
dejar disolver en la boca	dissolve on the tongue
disolver en agua	dissolve in water
dos/tres veces al día	twice/three times a day
en ayunas	on an empty stomach
para uso externo/interno	for external/internal use
sin masticar	swallow whole

At the dentist

I've got (terrible) toothache

Tengo dolores (fuertes) de muelas
[**tayn**go do**lo**rays (**fwayr**tays) day **mway**las]

I've lost a filling

Se me perdió un empaste
[say may payr**dee**o‿oon‿aym**pa**stay]

Could you

¿Puede [**pway**day]

see me immediately

atenderme ahora mismo
[atayn**dayr**may‿a**o**ra **mees**mo]

give me something for the
pain, please?

darme algo contra los dolores?
[**dar**may‿**al**go **kon**tra los do**lo**rays]

Could you give me an/
no injection, please

(No) Me ponga una inyección
[(no) may **pon**ga‿**oo**na‿eenyayk**thee**on]

Medical assistance

aids	sida *(m)* [**see**da]
allergy	alergia [a**layr**kheea]
antibiotic	antibiótico [antee**beeo**teeko]
appendicitis	apendicitis *(f)* [apayndee**thee**tees]
aspirin	aspirina [aspee**ree**na]
bleeding (strong)	hemorragia (fuerte) [aymora**khee**a (**fwayr**tay)]
burn	quemadura [kayma**doo**ra]
certificate	certificado [thayrteefee**ka**do]
circulatory problems	trastornos de la circulación [tras**tor**nos day la theerkoola**thee**on]
cold	constipado/resfriado [konstee**pa**do/ raysfree**a**do]
concussion	conmoción *(f)* cerebral [konmo**thee**on thayray**bral**]
constipation	estreñimiento [aystraynyeemee**ayn**to]
cough mixture	jarabe *(m)* pectoral [khara**bay** paykto**ral**]
disinfectant	desinfectante *(m)* [dayseenfayk**tan**tay]
diabetes	diabetes [deea**bay**tes]
diagnosis	diagnóstico [dee**agno**steeko]
eardrops	gotas para los oídos [**go**tas **pa**ra los o**ee**dos]
enteritis	entitis *(f)* [en**tee**tees]
eyedrops	gotas para los ojos [**go**tas **pa**ra los **o**khos]
flu	gripe *(f)* [**gree**pay]
fracture	fractura [frak**too**ra]
HIV-positive	VIH positivo [oovay‿ee‿a**chay** posee**tee**bo]
infectious	contagioso [kontakhee**o**so]
infection	infección *(f)* [eenfayk**thee**on]
inflammation	inflamación *(f)* [eenflama**thee**on]
injection	inyección *(f)* [eenyayk**thee**on]

Could you repair..., please	¡Repare..., por favor [rayparay... por favor]
the tooth	el diente [el deeayntay]
the bridge	el puente [el pwayntay]
the crown	la corona [la korona]
the filling	el empaste [el aympastay]
only temporarily!	sólo provisionalmente! [solo proveeseeonalmayntay]
Is it bad?	¿Es grave? [ays gravay]

At the hospital

Where is	¿Dónde está [donday⌣aysta]
a hospital	un hospital [oon⌣ospeetal]
the casualty department?	la ambulancia? [la⌣amboolantheea]

migraine	jaqueca [khakayka]
nausea	náuseas (f/pl) [naoosayas]
nurse	enfermera [aynfayrmayra]
ointment	pomada/ungüento (m) [pomada/oongooaynto]
operation	operación (f) [opayratheeon]
painkiller	analgésico [annalkhayseeko]
patient	paciente [patheeayntay]
plaster	esparadrapo [aysparadrapo]
poisoning	intoxicación (f) [eentoxeekatheeon]
pulled muscle	distensión (f) muscular [deestaynseeon mooskoolar]
pulled tendon	distorsión (f) de un tendón [deestorseeon day⌣oon tayndon]
pus	pus (m) [poos]
rash	erupción (f) cutánea [ayrooptheeon kootanaya]
seasickness	mal de mar [mal day mar]
sleeping pills	somnífero [somneefayro]
snake bite	picadura de serpiente [peekadoora day sayrpeeayntay]
sprain	distorsión (f) [deestorseeon]
sunstroke	insolación (f) [eensolatheeon]
sweat	sudor (m) [soodor]
swollen	hinchado [eenchado]
temperature	fiebre (f) [feeaybray]
tranquillizer	calmante (m) [kalmantay]
vaccination	vacuna [vakoona]
virus	virus (m) [veeroos]
vomiting	vómito [vomeeto]
wound	herida [ayreeda]
X-ray	una radiografía [oona radeeografeea]

PRACTICAL INFORMATION

Please call

Mr/Mrs...

at the... hotel!

Do you have private/
two-bed rooms?

What's the diagnosis?

Which treatment/therapy do
you propose?

How long will I have to stay?

When can I get up?

I feel (don't feel any) better

I need
a painkiller
sleeping pills.

Am I well enough to travel?

I'd like...
to see the doctor

to be discharged
a medical report

a certificate
for my medical insurance
for my doctor

At the pharmacy

I'm looking for a pharmacy

I have (I don't have) a
prescription

I need
something for a cough/
for a (head) ache

something for sunburn   .

for me
for adults
for children

Is the medicine strong/weak?

How many tablets/drops do I
have to take?

¡Avise *(sing)*/Avisen *(pl)* por favor
[aveesay/aveesayn por favor]
al señor/a la señora... [al saynyor/
a la saynyora]
en el hotel...! [ayn⌣ayl⌣otayl]
¿Hay cuartos privados/cuartos de dos camas?
[aee kwartos preebados/kwartos day dos kamas]
¿Cuál es el diagnóstico?
[kwal ays ayl deeagnosteeko]
¿Qué tratamiento/terapia propone?
[kay tratameeaynto/tayrapeea proponay]
¿Cuántos días tendré que quedarme?
[kwantos deeas tayndray kay kaydarmay]
¿Cuándo podré levantarme?
[kwando podray layvantarmay]
(No) Estoy mejor [(no) aystoy maykhor]

Necesito [naythayseeto]
un analgésico [oon ahnalkhayseeko]
un somnífero [oon somneefayro]
¿Puedo viajar? [pwaydo beeakhar]

Quería... [kayreea]
hablar con el médico
[ablar kon⌣ayl maydeeko]
que me den de alta [kay may⌣dayn day⌣alta]
un informe sobre el tratamiento
[oon eenformay sobray⌣ayl tratameeaynto]
un certificado [oon thayrteefeekado]
para mi seguro [para mee saygooro]
para el médico de cabecera
[para⌣ayl maydeeko day kabaythayra]

Estoy buscando una farmacia
[aystoy booskando⌣oona farmatheea]
(No) Tengo una receta
[(no) tayngo⌣oona raythayta]

¡Deme [daymay]
algo contra la tos/contra los dolores
(de cabeza)
[algo kontra la tos/kontra los dolorays
(day kabaytha)]
algo contra las quemaduras de sol
[algo kontra las kaymadooras day sol]
para mi! [para⌣mee]
para adultos! [para⌣adooltos]
para niños! [para⌣neenyos]
¿El medicamento es fuerte/suave?
[ayl maydeekamaynto⌣ays fwayrtay/swavay]
¿Cuántas pastillas/gotas tengo que tomar?
[kwantas pastee-yas/gotas tayngo kay tomar]

Could you give me a receipt/a copy of the prescription, please!	¡Por favor, deme [por favor daymay] un recibo/una copia de la receta! [oon raytheebo/oona kopeea day la raythayta]

Holidays and festivals

Is there a holiday/national holiday today?	¿Hoy es día de fiesta/fiesta Nacional? [oy ays deea day feeaysta/feeaysta natheeonal]
What's being celebrated today?	¿Qué fiesta se celebra hoy? [kay feeaysta say thaylaybra‿oy]
When does the festival start?	¿A qué hora empieza el programa festivo? [a kay‿ora aympeeaytha‿ayl programa faysteebo]
How long will it take?	¿Cuánto tiempo durará? [kwanto teeaympo doorara]
Where does the festival take place?	¿Dónde tiene lugar el espectáculo? [donday teeaynay loogar ayl ayspayktakoolo]

Money matters

Can I pay with ... here?	¿Puedo pagar aquí con [pwaydo pagar‿akee kon]
cheques	cheques [chaykays]
traveller's cheques	cheques de viaje [chaykays day beeakhay]
credit cards	tarjetas de crédito? [tarkhaytas day kraydeeto]
Where's the nearest	¿Dónde hay por aquí [donday aee por‿akee]
a bank/bureau de change	un banco/un cambio [oon banko/oon kambeeo]
a cash dispenser?	un cajero automático? [oon kakhero‿aootomateeko]
What time does the bank close?	¿A qué hora cierra el banco? [a kay‿ora theeayra ayl banko]
Can I withdraw money from my post office savings book here?	¿Puedo retirar aquí dinero de la libreta postal de ahorro? [pwaydo rayteerar‿akee deenayro day la leebrayta postal day‿aorro]

* ¿Cuánto quiere? [**kwan**to **kee**ayray]
30, 000 Pesetas

How much do you want?

Treinta mil pesetas [tray-**een**ta meel pay**say**tas]

What's the current exchange rate?

¿A cuánto está el cambio actual? [a **kwan**to ay**sta** ayl **kam**beeo⌣aktooal]

What's the maximum amount per cheque?

¿Cuál es el importe máximo por cheque? [kwal ays ayl eem**por**tay **max**eemo por **chay**kay]

How high are the charges per cheque? per transfer?

¿Hay una comisión [aee⌣**oo**na komeesee**on**] para los cheques [**para** los **chay**kays] para los giros? [**para** los **khee**ros]

I'd like to change 100 pounds sterling/dollars into pesetas, please

Quería cambiar cien libros ingleses/dollares en pesetas [kay**ree**a kam**beear** theeayn **lee**bros eeng**lay**says/**doll**arays ayn pay**say**tas]

Please give me some coins as well!

¡Deme también monedas, por favor! [**day**may tambee**ayn** mo**nay**das por fa**vor**]

* ¡Su tarjeta de cheques, por favor! [soo tar**khay**ta day **chay**kays por fa**vor**]

Can I see your cheque card, please?

* ¡Firme aquí, por favor! [**feer**may⌣a**kee** por fa**vor**]

Sign here, please!

Has my bank transfer/money order arrived yet?

¿Ha llegado mi giro bancario/postal? [a yay**ga**do mee **khee**ro ban**ka**reeo/po**stal**]

Crime and police

Where's the nearest police station?

¿Dónde está la comisaría más cercana? [**don**day⌣ay**sta** la komeesa**ree**a mas thayr**ka**na]

Please call the police!

¡Llame a la policía, por favor! [**ya**may⌣a la polee**thee**a por fa**vor**]

I've been
robbed
mugged on the road/ at the beach
This man is bothering/ following me

Me han [may⌣an]
robado [ro**ba**do]
asaltado en la calle/en la playa [asal**ta**do⌣ayn la **ka**yay/ayn la **pla**ya]
Este hombre me molesta/me persigue [**ay**stay⌣**om**bray may mo**lay**sta/may payr**see**gay]

My car has been broken into

Me han forzado la puerta del coche [may⌣an for**tha**do la **pwar**ta dayl **ko**chay]

...has been stolen!
My passport
My car
My bicycle
My wallet
My camera
My handbag
My cheques/cheque card

My watch

Me han robado [may⌣an ro**ba**do]
el pasaporte [ayl pasa**por**tay]
el coche [ayl **ko**chay]
la bicicleta [la beethee**klay**ta]
la cartera [la kar**tay**ra]
la cámara fotográfica [la **ka**mara foto**gra**feeka]
el bolso [ayl **bol**so]
los cheques/la tarjeta de cheques [los **chay**kays]/la tar**khay**ta day **chay**kays]
el reloj de pulsera [ayl ray**lokh** day pool**say**ra]

78

I'd like to report | Quería denunciar [kayreea daynoontheear]
a theft | un robo [oon **robo**]
a fraud | un fraude [oon **fraooday**]
a robbery | un atraco [oon a**tratho**]
a rape | una violación [**oo**na beeolathee**on**]

I'd like to speak to | Quería hablar [kayreea⌣a**blar**]
a lawyer | con un abogado [kon oon abo**gado**]
the (British/US) embassy | con la embajada (británico/americano) [kon la⌣emba**kha**da (breetaneeko/amayreekano)]

Does anyone here speak English? | ¿Hay alguien que hable inglés? [aee⌣al**geeayn** kay⌣ablay een**glays**]

I need | Necesito [naythay**seeto**]
an interpreter | un intérprete [oon een**tayr**praytay]
a written document for insurance purposes. | un certificado para mi seguro [oon thayrteefee**ka**do **pa**ra mee say**goo**ro]
It wasn't my fault | No tengo yo la culpa [no **tayn**go yo la **kool**pa]
I've got nothing to do with it | No tengo nada que ver con eso [no **tayn**go **na**da kay⌣vayr kon⌣**ay**so]

* ¿Cuándo/¿Dónde pasó? [**kwan**do/**don**day pa**so**] | When/Where did it happen?
* ¡Rellene esto, por favor! [rayaynay⌣**ay**sto por fa**vor**] | Fill this in, please!
* ¡Su dirección (aquí), por favor! [soo direk**theeon** (a**kee**) por fa**vor**] | Your address (here), please!

Emergencies

▶ *(See also* **breakdown, accident,** *page 25, and* **At the hospital,** *page 75)*

* ¡Atención! [atayn**theeon**] | Caution!
* ¡Peligro (de muerte)! [pay**lee**gro (day **mwayr**tay)] | (Serious) Danger!
* Salida de emergencia [sa**lee**da day⌣aymayr**khayn**theea] | Emergency exit
Help! | ¡Socorro! [so**korro**]

Opening times

When does... open/close? | ¿A qué hora abre/cierra [a kay⌣**ora**⌣abray/**theeay**ra]

the supermarket | el supermercado [ayl soopayrmayr**ka**do]
the department store | el almacén grande [ayl alma**thayn gran**day]
the shop | la tienda [la tee**ayn**da]
the bank/the post office | el banco/el correo [ayl **ban**ko/ayl ko**rayo**]
the museum? | el museo? [ayl moo**sayo**]
Are you open at lunch time? | ¿Está abierto a mediodía? [ay**sta**⌣abee**ayr**to⌣a maydeeo**dee**a]

Is there a day you are closed? | ¿Hay un día de descanso? [aee⌣oon **dee**a day days**kan**so]

Post office

Where can I find
a post office
a post-box?

Por favor, ¿dónde está [por favor donday‿aysta]
el correo [ayl korayo]
un buzón? [oon boothon]

I'd like
10 stamps/special issue
stamps
for postcards/letters
to England/the United
States
a phonecard, please!

¡**Deme** [**day**may]
diez sellos/sellos especiales
[dee-ayth **say**os/**say**os ayspaythee**a**lays]
para postales/cartas [para posta**lays/kar**tas]
a Inglaterra/a los Estados Unidos
[a‿eenglatayra/a los aystados ooneedos]
una tarjeta telefónica, por favor!
[oona tarkhayta taylayfoneeka por favor]

By airmail/Express, please
Registered, please
* Lista de correos
[**lee**sta day korayos]
Do you have any mail for me?
I would like to send a packet/
a telegram

Por avión/Urgente [por‿avee**on**/oor**khayn**tay]
Certificada [thayrteefee**ka**da]
Poste restante

¿Hay correo para mí? [aee korayo para‿mee]
Quería enviar un pequeño paquete/un
telegrama [kayreea‿enveear oon paykaynyo
pakaytay/oon taylaygrama]

How much do you charge for
ten words?
Can I send a fax to... from
here?
How much is one page?

¿Cuánto cuestan diez palabras?
[**kwan**to **kway**stan day-eeth palabras]
¿Puedo mandar un telefax a...?
[**pway**do man**dar** oon taylay**fax** a]
¿Cuánto cuesta una página?
[**kwan**to **kway**sta‿oona pakheena]

Radio and television

**On which wavelength can I
pick up**
the traffic report

English radio programmes?

What time is the news?

Do you have a TV guide?

What channels do you get?

¿**En qué frecuencia se sintoniza**
[ayn kay fray**kooayn**theea say seentoneetha]
la información viaria?
[la‿eenforma**theeon** veeareea]
emisiones de radio en en inglés?
[aymee**seeo**nays day **ra**deeo ayn‿een**glays**]
¿A qué hora hay las noticias?
[a kay‿ora‿aee las no**tee**theeas]
¿Tiene un programa de la tele?
[tee**ay**nay‿oon pro**gra**ma day la **tay**lay]
¿Qué programas hay? [kay **pro**gramas aee]

Telecommunications

(Where) can I
make a phone call
buy a phonecard?

¿**(Dónde) Puedo** [(donday) **pway**do]
telefonear [taylayfona**yar**]
comprar una tarjeta telefónica?
[kom**prar** oona tar**khay**ta taylayfoneeka]

Is there... around here?
a public phone

¿**Hay por aquí** [aee por‿akee]
un teléfono público [oon tay**lay**fono
poobleeko]

a payphone/cardphone	un teléfono de monedas/de tarjeta [oon taylayfono day monaydas/day tarkhayta]
a public phonebox where I can receive calls?	una cabina dónde me pueden llamar a mí? [oona kabeena donday may pwaydayn yamar a mee]
How do I make an outside call?	¿Cómo hago una llamada al exterior? [como ago oona yamada al extereeor]
I'd like to make a phone call to England/the United States/Canada/Australia/New Zealand/Ireland	Quería llamar a Inglaterra/los Estados Unidos/Canadá/Australia/Nueva Zelanda/Irlanda [kayreea yamar a_eenglatayra/los aystados ooneedos/canada/aoostraleea/nooayba thaylanda/eerlanda]
Can I dial directly?	¿Hay servicio directo? [aee sayrbeetheeo deeraykto]
What is the area code?	¿Cuál es el prefijo? [kwal ays ayl prayfeekho]
Can you change this?	¿Puede darme cambio? [pwayday darmay kambeeo]
I need coins for the telephone	Necesito monedas para el teléfono [naythayseeto monaydas para_ayl taylayfono]
A long-distance call to..., please!	¡Una llamada a larga distancia con...! [oona yamada_a larga deestantheea kon]
Is there a long waiting time?	¿Tengo que esperar mucho? [tayngo kay_ayspayrar moocho]
What's the charge per minute?	¿Cuánto cuesta un minuto? [kwanto kwaysta_oon meenooto]
Is there a cheap rate at night time?	¿Hay una tarifa reducida de noche? [aee_oona tareefa raydootheeda day nochay]
I'd like to make a reversed charge call	Una llamada a cobro revertido, por favor [oona yamada_a kobro rayvayrteedo por favor]
* ¡Ocupado!/Están comunicando [okoopado/aystan komooneekando]	Engaged
There's no reply	No contestan [no kontaystan]
* ¡Díga!/¡Dígame! [deega/deegamay]	Hello!
I can't hear you	No le oigo [no lay oeego]
Can you hear me?	¿Me oye? [may oyay]
I must have dialled the wrong number	He marcado el número incorrecto [hay markado ayl noomayro eencoraykto]
Hello, this is...	Buenos días, soy... [bwaynos deeas soy]
Can I speak to Mr/Mrs... ?	¿Puedo hablar con el señor/la señora...? [pwaydo_ablar kon ayl saynyor/la saynyora]
* Al aparato [al_aparato]	Speaking
* Lo siento, pero no está [lo seeaynto payro no_aysta]	Sorry, he/she is not here at the moment
Do you speak English?	¿Habla inglés? [abla_eenglays]
When is he/she back?	¿Cuándo estará? [kwando_aystara]
I'll call again later	Llamo otra vez más tarde [yamo otra vayth mas tarday]
Please tell him/her that I called	Dígale por favor que he llamado [deegalay por favor kay_ay yamado]
My number is...	Mi número es... [mee noomayro_es]

Making phone calls

As in Britain, the Spanish postal service (*Correos*) and the national telephone company (*Telefónica*) are not linked.

If you want to make a long-distance phone call from a public payphone (*cabina telefónica*), then you will need either a good supply of 100 peseta coins or a telephone card (*tarjeta telefónica* or *tarjeta prepago*), which can be purchased from supermarkets and tobacconists. Most payphones have instructions in several languages. Lift the receiver, wait for the tone, deposit the minimum number of coins necessary, and then dial the relevant number, omitting the initial zero of the city code you require.

Practically all cafés and restaurants also have public telephones with unit counters, where you may talk as long as you wish and pay up later. Units will cost a little more than when you make a call from a *Telefónica* payphone. In many larger cities there are now licensed telephone shops (*locutorios*), from where long-distance calls are very much cheaper than phoning home via the hotel switchboard.

When you want to make an international call, first dial the 07 international call code, wait for the dialling tone and then key in the relevant country code as follows:

Australia 00 61
Canada 00 1
New Zealand 00 64
United Kingdom 00 44
Republic of Ireland 00 353
United States 00 1

Can I receive email from here?	¿Se puede recibir por correo electrónico? [say **pway**day raythee**beer** por cor**ay**o electron**i**co]
Can I send emails from here?	¿Puedo mandarle algo por correo electrónico? [**pway**do mandar**lay al**go por cor**ay**o electron**i**co]
Is there an internet café near here?	¿Hay algún internet bar cerca de aqui? [Aee alg**oon een**tayrnayt bar **thay**rka day akee]

Toilets

Where are the toilets please?	¿Dónde están los lavabos, por favor? [**don**day⌣ay**stan** los lava**bos** por fa**vor**]
Is there a public toilet around here?	¿Hay lavabos públicos por aquí? [aee lava**bos poo**bleekos por⌣a**kee**]
* Señoras (Damas)/Señores (Caballeros) [say**nyo**ras (**da**mas)/saynyo**rays** (kaba**lyay**ros)]	Ladies/Gentlemen

Tipping

Is service included?	¿El servicio está incluído? [ayl sayr**bee**theeo aysta⌣eenkloo**ee**do]
How much does one tip?	¿Cuánto se da de propina? [**kwan**to say da day prop**ee**na]
That's for you! Keep the change!	¡Es para usted! [ays **para**⌣oo**stay**] ¡Quédese con el resto! [**kay**daysay kon ayl **ray**sto]
That's fine!	Está bien así [ay**sta** bee-ayn⌣a**see**]

82

English–Spanish A–Z

A

about cerca [**thay**rka]
accident el accidente
[akthee**dayn**tay] 25, 27
accidentally por descuido [por
daysk**wee**do]
accommodation el alojamiento
[alokhamee**ayn**to] 32, 38
address la dirección
[deerayk**thee**on] 15, 79
admission (ticket) la entrada
[ayn**tra**da] 52, 58
adult el adulto [a**doo**lto] 29, 52
advance ticket sales la venta
anticipada [**vayn**ta anteethee**pa**da] 59
afternoon por la tarde [por la **tar**de] 19
age la edad [ay**da**] 15
agreed vale [**ba**lay]
air conditioning el aire acondicionado
[a-**ee**ray akondeethee**o**nado] 38
air bed el colchón neumático [kol**chon**
nayooma**tee**ko] 53
air el aire [a**ee**ray] 20, 26
airport el aeropuerto
[a-ayro**pwayr**to] 22, 31
alarm clock el despertador
[dayspayrta**dor**] 67
alone solo/-a [**so**lo/-a]
always siempre [see**aym**pray]
ambulance la ambulancia
[amboo**lan**theea] 25, 72
angry furioso/-a [foo**ree**oso/-a]
animal el animal [ani**mal**] 36
answer machine el contestador
automático [kontaysta**dor**
aooto**ma**teeko] 82
antiques las antigüedades
[anteeg**we**dadays] 69
apartment el piso [**pee**so] 35
appointment la cita [**thee**ta]
bull ring la plaza de toros [**pla**tha day
toros] 50
arm el brazo [**bra**tho] 73
art gallery la galería de arte
[galay**ree**a day **ar**tay] 52
aunt la tía [**tee**a] 13
autumn el otoño [o**to**nyo] 18
avenue la alameda [ala**may**da]

B

baby el bebé [be**bay**]
baby's bottle el biberón
[beebay**ron**] 70, 71
babysitter el/la canguro [kan**goo**ro]
bachelor el soltero [sol**tay**ro] 14
bad malo/-a [**ma**lo/-a]
bakery la panadería [panaday**ree**a] 61
ball (dance) el baile [**ba**eelay] 15
ball la pelota [pay**lo**ta] 55
bandage (vb) vendar [**vayn**dar] 72
bank el banco [**ban**ko] 64, 77
bar la tasca [**ta**ska] 40
bath el baño [**ba**nyo] 33
battery la batería [bate**ree**a] 26, 67
bay la bahía [ba**ee**a] 55
beach la playa [**pla**eeya] 32, 53
beautiful bello/-a [**bay**o/-a]
beauty salon el salón de belleza
[sa**lon** day bay-**yay**tha]
bed la cama [**ka**ma] 38
beer la cerveza [thayr**bay**tha] 48
belt el cinturón [theentoo**ron**] 67
bicycle la bicicleta
[beethee**klay**ta] 22, 26
bill (the), please! ¡La cuenta, por
favor! [la **kwayn**ta por favor] 43
bill la cuenta [**kwayn**ta] 35, 43
birthday el cumpleaños
[koompla**yan**yos] 14, 18
bit (a), un poco [un **po**ko]
blame la culpa [**kool**pa] 79
blanket la manta [**man**ta] 35
blood la sangre [**san**gray] 74
boat la barca [**bar**ka] 53
body el cuerpo [**kwayr**po] 74
book el libro [**lee**bro] 64
bookshop la librería
[leebray**ree**a] 64
boots las botas [**bo**tas] 67
border la frontera [fron**tay**ra]
boring aburrido/-a [aboo**ree**do/-a]
born nacido/-a [na**thee**do/-a] 18
bottle opener el abridor [abree**dor**] 61
bottle la botella [bo**ta**ya] 42, 64
bowl la fuente [**fwayn**tay]
boy el chico [**chee**ko]
breakdown la avería [ava**ree**a] 25

breakfast el desayuno
[daysayoono] 33
bridge el puente [**pwayn**tay] 50, 75
bright claro/-a [**klaro**/-a] 20
broadcast la emisión [aymeeseeon] 80
broken roto/-a [**roto**/-a] 67
brother el hermano [ayr**mano**] 13
brother-in-law el cuñado
[koon**yado**] 13
bureau de change el cambio
[**kambeeo**] 77
burn (n) quemadura [kaymadoora]
bus stop la parada [parada] 28
bus el autobús [auto**boos**] 16, 29
butcher la carnicería
[karneethay**reea**] 61
button el botón [boton] 61
buy (vb) comprar [kom**prar**] 61

C
cabin la cabina [kabeena] 31
café el bar [bar] 40
cake-shop la pastelería
[pastaylay**reea**] 40
call (vb) llamar [yamar]
called, to be llamarse [yamar**say**] 32
calm el silencio [seelayn**theeo**] 16
camera la cámara fotográfica [**kamara**
fotografeeka] 68, 79
camper van la autocaravana
[aootokaravana] 22, 36
campsite el camping [kam**peeng**] 36
cap la gorra [**gora**] 67
car el coche [**koch**ay] 22, 26
caravan la caravana
[karavana] 36
carnival la fiesta popular
[fee**aysta** popoo**lar**] 60
carpark el aparcamiento
[aparkamee**aynto**] 24, 34
cash desk la caja [**kakha**] 59
cash el dinero en efectivo
[dee**nayro** ayn ayfayk**teebo**] 77
castle el castillo [kas**teelyo**] 50
cat el gato [**gato**] 36
cathedral la catedral [katay**dral**] 52
cause la razón [rathon] 14
ceiling/roof el techo [**taycho**] 32
centre el centro [**thayn**tro] 22, 28
certificate el certificado
[thayrteefee**kado**] 76, 79
chair la silla [**seeya**] 40
change (vb) cambiar [kambee**ar**] 30

chapel la capilla [kapeeya] 50
charge (in) responsable
[rayspon**sablay**]
charge el coste (s) [**kostay**] 78
charter flight el vuelo chárter [vwaylo
chartayr] 30
cheap barato/-a [barato/-a] 61
cheeky descarado/-a [daykarado/-a]
chemist la farmacia [farmatheea] 76
cheque el cheque [**chaykay**] 78
child el/la niño/-a [neenyo/-a] 13
Christmas Navidad [nabeedad] 14, 60
church la iglesia [eeglayseea] 52
cigarette el cigarrillo [theegareeyo] 71
cinema el cine [**theenay**] 15, 57
circular walk la vuelta [vwaylta] 49
clean limpio/-a [**leempeeo**/-a]
clock el reloj [raylokh] 67, 79
closed cerrado/-a [thayrado/-a] 80
clothing los vestidos
[baysteedos] 65, 67
coast la costa [**kosta**] 53
coat el abrigo [abreego] 65
coins la moneda [monayda] 82
cold frío/-a [freeo/-a] 20, 42
colour el color [kolor] 20, 65
comb el peine [**payeenay**] 71
company la empresa [aym**praysa**]
compensation la indemnización
[eendaymneethatheeon] 25
complaint la queja [**kaykha**] 42
concert el concierto [kontheeayrto] 57
condom el condón/el preservativo
[kondon/praysayrbateebo] 71
confuse confundir [konfoondeer]
congratulate felicitar
[fayleetheetar] 14
connection el enlace [aynlathay] 29
contraceptive el anticonceptivo
[anteekonthaypteebo] 71
contract el contrato [kontrato]
cook el/la cocinero/-a
[kotheenayro/-a] 40
corkscrew el sacacorchos
[sakakorchos] 61
correct correcto/-a [korraykto/-a]
cost (vb) costar [kostar] 16, 31
costs los gastos [**gastos**]
cotton wool el algodón [algodon] 61
cotton el algodón [algodon] 65
couchette el coche-literas [**kochay**
leetayras] 29
counter la ventanilla [bayntaneeya]

country house la finca (rústica)
[**feen**ka (**roos**teeka)] 32
country el país [pa-**ees**] 69
countryside el paisaje
[paee**sak**hay] 51
cousin el/la primo/-a [**preem**o/-a] 13
credit card la tarjeta de crédito
[tar**khay**ta day **kray**deeto] 77
cruise el crucero [kroo**thay**ro] 31
cry (vb) llorar [yo**rar**]
culture la cultura [kool**too**ra] 49, 57
cup la taza [**tath**a] 43
currency la moneda [mo**nay**da] 77
customs la aduana [a**doo**ana] 21, 22
cutlery el cubierto [koobee**ayr**to] 43

D

damp húmedo/-a [**oom**aydo/-a]
dance (vb) bailar [bae**e**lar] 15, 60
dance el baile [**bae**elay] 15
danger el peligro [pay**lee**gro] 54
dark oscuro/-a [os**koo**ro/-a] 20
date la fecha [**fay**cha] 18
daughter la hija [**eek**ha] 13
day el día [**dee**a] 15
deep profundo/-a [pro**foo**ndo/-a]
degree el grado [**gra**do] 20
dentist el dentista [dayn**tees**ta] 72, 74
deodorant el desodorante
[desodo**ran**tay] 71
department store el almacén grande
[alma**thayn gran**day] 80
department el departamento
[daypart**ama**ynto] 29
departure la partida [par**teed**a] 28, 29
deposit la caución [kaoothee**on**] 23
dessert el postre [**pos**tray] 47
destination la meta [**may**ta] 54
diesel el gasoil [**gas**oeel] 24
difference la diferencia
[deefay**rayn**theea]
different diferente [deefay**rayn**tay]
difficult difícil [dee**fee**theel]
direct directo/-a [dee**rayk**to/-a]
direction la dirección
[deerayk**thee**on] 28
director el/la director/-a
[deerayk**tor**/-a]
dirty sucio/-a [**soo**theeo/-a] 34
disabled minusválido/-a
[meenoos**bal**eedo/-a] 72
discotheque la discoteca
[deesko**tay**ka] 58

discount el descuento
[days**kwayn**to] 61
district el barrio [**bar**eeo] 22
diversion el desvío [days**bee**o]
dizzy mareado/-a [mara**yad**o/-a] 72
doctor el/la médico/-a
[**may**deeko/-a] 25, 72
dog el perro [**pay**ro]
donkey el burro [**boo**ro]
door la puerta [**pwayr**ta]
doubt (n) la duda [**doo**da]
dream (vb) soñar [**so**nyar]
drink (vb) beber [bay**bayr**] 15
drink la bebida [bay**beed**a] 42, 48
drinking water el agua (f) potable
[**ag**ooa po**tab**lay] 39
driver el conductor [kondook**tor**] 27
driver's licence el carné de conducir
[**kar**nay day kondoo**theer**] 21
drugstore la droguería
[droga**yree**a] 70, 71
drunk borracho [bo**rach**o]
dry cleaner's la tintorería
[teento**ra**yreea] 67
dry cleaning el lavado en seco
[la**vad**o (ayn **say**ko)] 67
dummy el chupete [choo**pay**tay] 70, 71

E

early temprano [taym**pra**no] 18
earn ganar [ga**nar**]
earrings los pendientes
[payndee**ayn**tays] 67
earth la tierra [tee**ayr**a]
east el este [**ays**tay] 22
Easter Páscua [**pas**kwa] 14
easy fácil [**fath**eel]
edible comestible [komays**teeb**lay]
education la educación
[aydooka**thee**on]
electrical store los electrodomésticos
[aylayktrodo**mays**teekos] 68
electricity la electricidad
[aylayktree**theed**a] 36, 39
embassy la embajada [aymba**kha**da]
emergency brake el freno de alarma
[**fray**no day a**lar**ma] 27, 29
emergency exit la salida de
emergencia [sa**leed**a day
(aymayrk**hay**ntheea) 79
emergency phone el poste de socorro
[**pos**tay day so**ko**ro] 79
empty vacío/-a [ba**thee**o/-a]

engine el motor [**motor**] 26, 27
England Inglaterra [eenglat**ayra**] 13
English (person) inglesa
  [eengl**ays**a] 13, 52
English (language) inglés
  [eengl**ays**] 13, 52
enter! ¡Adelante!/¡Pase!
  [aday**lan**tay/**pas**ay]
entertainment el divertimiento
  [deebayrteemee**ayn**to] 57, 59
entrance la entrada [ayn**trada**]
environmental protection la
  protección del medio ambiente
  [protaykthee**on** dayl **may**deeo
  ambee**ayn**tay] 56
evening la tarde [**tar**day] 12
events calendar el calendario de
  actos [kalayn**dareeo** dayl **ak**tos] 49
everything todo [**todo**]
excursion la excursión [la
  exkoorsee**on**] 52
exhausted agotado/-a [a**go**tado/-a]
exit la salida [sa**lee**da]
expensive caro/-a [**karo**/-a] 61
extend prolongar [prolon**gar**]
extinguisher el extintor
  [ayx**teentor**] 79

F

factory la fábrica [**fabreeka**]
faithful fiel [fee**ayl**]
family la familia [fa**meeleea**] 12
fan el aficionado [afeethee**onado**] 54
fashion la moda [**moda**] 65
fast rápido/-a [**rapeedo**/-a]
father el padre [**padray**] 13
faulty estropeado/-a [aystropa**yado**/-a]
  27, 34
fax el telefax [taylay**fax**] 80
fear el miedo [mee**aydo**] 72, 78
fee los derechos [dayray**chos**] 78
few a poco/-a [**poko**/-a]
field el campo [**kampo**] 56
fine (penalty) la multa [**moolta**]
finger el dedo [**daydo**] 73
fire brigade los bomberos
  [bomb**ayros**] 25
fire el fuego [fw**aygo**] 79
fishmonger la pescadería
  [payskaday**reea**] 64
flash (photo) el flash [**flash**] 68
flat el piso [**peeso**] 35
flea-market el rastro [**rastro**] 61

flight departure el despegue
  [days**payg**way] 30
flight el vuelo [vw**aylo**] 30
flirt el mariposón [maree**poson**]
floor el suelo [sw**aylo**]
flower la flor [**flor**]
fly la mosca [**moska**]
food los comestibles
  [komays**teeblays**] 62, 64
foot el pie [**peeay**] 74
football el fútbol [**footbol**] 55
forbidden prohibido/-a
  [proee**beedo**/-a]
foreigner el/la extranjero/-a
  [estran**khayro**/-a] 15
forget olvidar [olbee**dar**]
fork el tenedor [taynay**dor**] 43
form el impreso [eem**prayso**] 21, 78
fragile frágil [**frakheel**]
free of charge gratis [**gratees**]
free libre [**leebray**]
fresh fresco/-a [**fraysko**/-a]
Friday el viernes [bee**ayrnays**] 18
friend el/la amigo/-a
  [a**meego**/-a] 12, 14
fruit la fruta [**froota**] 62
full board la pensión completa
  [paynsee**on** kom**playta**] 33
full up repleto [ray**playto**]
full lleno/-a [**yayno**/-a]
furniture los muebles [**mwayblays**]
fuse el fusible [foo**seeblay**] 26

G

garage el garage [gara**khay**] 34, 38
garden el jardín [khar**deen**]
garment el vestido [bay**steedo**] 65
girl la chica [**cheeka**]
glass (of wine) la copa [**kopa**] 42, 43
glass (pane of) el vidrio [**beedreeo**] 50
glass (tumbler) el vaso [**baso**] 43
glove los guantes [gw**antays**] 67
go (vb) ir [**eer**]
good bueno/-a [**bweno**/-a];
  (adv) bien [bee-**ayn**]
government el gobierno [gobee**ayrno**]
gram el gramo [**gramo**] 19, 64
grandfather/grandmother
  el/la abuelo/-a [abw**aylo**/-a] 13
grandson el/la nieto/-a
  [nee**ayto**/-a] 13
greengrocer la frutería
  [frootay**reea**] 61

greet saludar [saloo**dar**] 12, 13
ground-floor la planta baja [**plan**ta
  bakha] 32
group el grupo [**groo**po]
guard el revisor [rayvee**sor**]
guided tour la visita
  [bee**see**ta] 49, 52

H

hair el pelo/el cabello [**pay**lo/kaba-yo]
  70
hairdresser el/la peluquero/-a
  [paylook**ay**ro/-a]
half medio/-a [**may**deeo/-a]
handbag el bolso [**bol**so]
handicrafts la artesanía
  [artaysan**ee**-a] 69
happy feliz [fay**leeth**]
hard difícil [deefee**theel**]
hard duro/-a [**doo**ro/-a]
hat el sombrero [sombr**ay**ro] 67
have, to have tener [tay**nayr**]
head la cabeza [ka**bay**tha]
health la salud [sa**loo**] 72
healthy sano/-a [**sa**no/-a]
heating la calefacción
  [kalayfakthe**on**] 34, 38
heavy pesado/-a [pay**sa**do/-a]
hello! ¡Hola! [**o**la] 12, 13
help (vb) ayudar [ayoo**dar**] 25
help! ¡Socorro! [so**ko**ro] 14, 27
high alto/-a [**al**to/-a]
highway la carretera [karay**tay**ra] 21
hike (vb) hacer excursiones [a**thayr**
  eskoorsee**on**ays] 56
hobby la afición [afeethe**on**]
holiday (public) el día festivo [**dee**a
  fay**stee**bo] 77
holiday las vacaciones
  [bakathe**on**es] 14
home (native land) la patria [**pat**reea]
home, at en casa [en **ka**sa]
hope (vb) esperar [ayspay**rar**]
hospital el hospital [ospee**tal**] 75
hot caliente [kalee**ayn**tay] 20, 42
hotel el hotel [o**tayl**] 32
hour la ora [**o**ra] 19, 24
house la casa [**ka**sa] 35
household goods los artículos
  domésticos [ar**tee**koolos
  domay**stee**kos] 61
hunger el hambre (f) [**am**bray] 40
husband el marido [ma**ree**do] 12

I

identity card el carné de identidad
  [kar**nay** day eedaynte**edad**] 21
identity card el documento de
  identidad [dokoo**mayn**to day
  eedaynte**edad**] 21, 79
ill enfermo/-a [ayn**fayr**mo/-a] 72
important importante [eempor**tan**tay]
impossible imposible [eempo**see**blay]
in writing por escrito [por es**kree**to]
including incluído/-a [eenkloo**eed**o/-a] 83
information la información
  [eenformathe**on**] 49
inhabitant el/la habitante
  [abee**tan**tay]
injured herido/-a [ay**reed**o/-a] 25
innocent inocente [eeno**thayn**tay] 78
insurance el seguro [say**goo**ro] 25, 79
intelligent inteligente
  [eentaylee**khayn**tay]
interesting interesante
  [eentayrays**an**tay] 52
interpreter el/la intérprete
  [een**tayr**praytay]
invalid no válido [no **bal**eedo] 21, 27
investigation el examen
  [es**am**ayn] 72, 78
island la isla [**ees**la] 50

J

jacket la chaqueta [cha**kay**ta] 65
jeans los tejanos [tay**khan**os] 67
jellyfish la medusa [may**doo**sa] 53
jersey el jersey [khayr**say**] 65
jewellery las joyas [**kho**yas] 67-69
jogging suit el chándal [**chan**dal] 67
joke la broma [**bro**ma]
judgement el juicio [khoo**ee**theeo]
jungle la selva [**sayl**ba] 56

K

key la llave [**ya**vay] 34, 39
kilo el kilo [**kee**lo] 19, 64
kilometre el kilómetro
  [kee**lo**maytro] 16, 23
kiosk el kiosko [kee**os**ko] 61
kiss (vb) besar [bay**sar**]
kiss el beso [**bay**so]
knife el cuchillo [koo**chee**yo] 43

L

ladies las señoras [sayn**yo**ras]
ladies' toilet damas [**dam**as] 83

lake el lago [**lago**] 50
landing el aterrizaje [atayree**thakh**ay] 30
landlord el patrón [pat**ron**] 39
language la lengua [**layn**gwa]
large grande [**granday**]
laundry la lavandería [lavanday**reea**] 67
lawn el césped [**thays**payd]
lazy perezoso/-a [payray**thoso**/-a]
leather el cuero [**kwayro**] 65, 69
left luggage office la consigna [kon**seeg**na] 30
left a la izquierda [a la eethkee**ayr**da]
left-luggage locker la consigna automática [kon**seeg**na aooto**mat**eeka] 30
leg la pierna [pee**ayr**na] 73
length la longitud [lonkhee**tood**] 19
letter la carta [**karta**] 80
letterbox el buzón [boo**thon**] 80
life-jacket el chaleco salvavidas [cha**layk**o salba**beed**as] 53
lift el ascensor [asthayn**sor**] 39
light (weight) ligero/-a [lee**khay**ro/-a]
light la luz [**looth**] 34, 39
linen el lino [**leeno**] 65
lipstick un pintalabios [peenta**lab**eeos] 70
live (vb) vivir [bee**beer**] 32
local train el tren de cercanías [trayn day thayrka**neea**s] 29
lock la cerradura [thayra**doo**ra] 34
long largo/-a [**lar**go/-a]
look for buscar [boos**kar**]
lorry el camión [kamee**on**] 22
lost property office la oficina de objetos perdidos [ofee**theen**a day ob**khay**tos payr**deed**os] 78
loud alto/-a [**alt**o/-a] 34
love (vb) amar [a**mar**]
love el amor [a**mor**]
low bajo/-a [**bakh**o/-a]
luggage trolley el carrito (para equipajes) [ka**reet**o (**para** aykee**pakh**ays)] 29
luggage el equipaje [aykee**pakh**ay] 39
lunch el almuerzo [almoo**ayr**tho] 17, 40

M

magazine la revista [ray**veest**a] 70
make-up el maquillaje [makee**yakh**ay] 70

man el hombre [**om**bray], el señor [sayn**yor**] 12
many mucho/-a [**moocho**/-a]
map el mapa [**mapa**] 49, 65
market el mercado [mayr**kado**] 51
married casado/-a [ka**sado**/-a] 14
matches las cerillas [thay**ree**yas] 71
material la tela [**tayla**] 61
meal el plato [**plato**] 42
meal la comida [ko**meeda**] 40, 73
medicine el medicamento [maydeeka**maynto**] 73
menu la carta [**karta**] 41, 45
metre el metro [**maytro**] 19
midday el mediodía [maydeeo**deea**] 17, 19
minute el minuto [mee**nooto**] 17, 82
misfortune la desgracia [days**grath**eea] 25, 53
mistake el error [ay**ror**]
modern moderno/-a [mo**dayrno**/-a]
moment el momento [mo**maynto**] 14
monastery el monasterio [monas**tayreeo**] 51
Monday el lunes [**loonays**] 18
money el dinero [dee**nayro**] 34, 77
month el mes [**mays**] 18, 19
morning la mañana [man**yana**] 19
mosquito el mosquito [mos**keeto**] 72
mother la madre [**madray**] 13
motorcycle la moto [**moto**] 22, 26
motorway (toll) la autopista (de peaje) [aooto**peesta** (day pay**akh**ay)] 22, 24
mountain la montaña [mon**tanya**] 51, 56
much mucho/-a [**moocho**/-a]
music la música [**mooseeka**] 57, 58

N

nail file la lima de uñas [**leema** day **oonyas**] 71
nail varnish el esmalte [ays**maltay**] 70
naked desnudo/-a [days**noodo**/-a]
name el nombre [**nombray**] 25, 40
nappies los pañales [pan**yalays**] 70, 71
nationality la nacionalidad [natheeonalee**dad**]
nature la naturaleza [natoora**laytha**] 56
necessary necesario [naythay**sareeo**]
nephew el sobrino [so**breeno**] 13
never jamás [kha**mas**]
New Year el Año Nuevo [**anyo** nooay**bo**] 14, 60

new nuevo/-a [nooaybo/-a]
news las noticias [noteetheeas] 82
newspaper el periódico
  [payreeodeeko] 61, 64
niece la sobrina [sobreena] 13
night la noche [nochay] 12, 19
no no [no]
nobody nadie [nadeeay]
noise el ruido [rooeedo] 34
noisy inquieto/-a [eenkeeayto/-a]
non-smoker no fumadores [no
  foomadorays] 30, 31
normal normal [normal]
north el norte [nortay] 22
not no [no]
notary el notario [notareeo] 79
nothing nada [nada]
nothing, it's (not at all) de nada [day
  nada]
number el número [noomero] 31, 41

O
obvious claro/-a [klaro/-a]
occupied ocupado [okoopado] 24
office la oficina (pública) [ofeetheena
  (poobleeka)] 80
OK vale [balay]
old viejo/-a [beeaykho/-a]
open abierto/-a [abeeayrto/-a] 79
opening times las horas de apertura
  [oras day apayrtoora] 52, 79
optician el óptico [opteeko] 69
other otro/-a [otro/-a]
owner el/la dueño/a
  [dwaynyo/-a] 32, 40

P
page la página [pakheena] 80
pain el dolor [dolor] 76
palace el palacio [palatheeo] 52
papers los papeles [papaylays] 21
parasol la sombrilla/el parasol
  [sombreeya/parasol] 53
parcel el pequeño paquete [paykaynyo
  pakaytay] 80
parents los padres [padrays] 13
park el parque [parkay] 51
part la parte [partay]
party la fiesta [feeaysta] 60, 77
passage el paso [paso] 22
passport el pasaporte [pasaportay] 21
past el pasado [pasado]
path el camino [kameeno] 22, 56

pay pagar [pagar] 43, 64
pedestrian el peatón [payaton]
people el pueblo [pwayblo], la gente
  [khayntay]
per thousand por mil [por meel] 78
perfume el perfume [payrfoomay] 71
perhaps tal vez [tal bayth]
person el hombre [ombray]
petrol station la gasolinera
  [gasoleenayra] 24, 25
petrol la gasolina [gasoleena] 23, 24
picture el cuadro [kwadro] 51
piece la pieza [peeaytha] 64
pillow la almohada [almo-ada] 35, 39
place el lugar [loogar] 22
plain la llanura [yanoora] 56
plant la planta [planta] 56
plate el plato [plato] 43
platform el andén [andayn] 29
please por favor [por favor]
poisonous (substance) tóxico/a
  [toxeeko/-a]
poisonous venenoso/-a
  [vaynaynoso/-a]
police la policía [poleetheea] 25, 78
policeman el policía
  [poleetheea] 25, 78
politics la política [poleeteeka]
poor pobre [pobray]
port el puerto [pwayrto] 22, 31
possible posible [poseeblay]
postcard la tarjeta postal [tarkhayta
  postal] 70
postcode el código postal [kodeego
  postal] 80
powder los polvos [polbos] 70
pregnant embarazada
  [embarathada] 73
present el regalo [raygalo] 21
preservative el preservativo
  [praysayrbateebo] 71
pretty bonito/-a [boneeto/-a]
price el precio [pretheeo] 83
probably probablemente
  [probablaymayntay]
profession la profesión
  [profayseeon] 15
programme el programa
  [programa] 58, 80
pull! ¡Tire! [teeray]
pullover el jersey [khayrsay] 65
punishment el castigo [kasteego]
purse el monedero [monaydayro] 77

Q

quality la calidad [kaleedad] 40, 61
question la pregunta [praygoonta] 16
quiet tranquilo [trankeelo]
quietly bajo/-a [bakho/-a]

R

rain la lluvia [yoobeea] 20
rape la violación [beeolatheeon] 79
razor blade las hojas de afeitar [okhas
    day afayeetar] 71
ready listo/-a [leesto/-a]
reason la razón [rathon]
receipt el recibo [raytheebo] 43, 77
reception la recepción
    [raythayptheeon] 32
recipe la receta [raythayta]
record el disco [deesko] 61
relative el/la pariente [pareeayntay] 13
repeat repetir [raypayteer]
restaurant el restaurante
    [raystaoorantay] 40, 49
return (vb) volver [bolbayr]
rich rico/-a [reeko/-a]
right a la derecha [a la dayraycha]
risk el riesgo [reeaysgo] 22, 53
river el río [reeo] 56
road sign la señal [saynyal] 23
room (hotel) la sala [sala] 32, 49
room el cuarto [kwarto] 32, 33
rubbish la basura [basoora] 39
rucksack la mochila [mocheela] 56

S

sad triste [treestay]
safe seguro/-a [saygooro/-a]
safety belt el cinturón de seguridad
    [theentooron day saygooreedad] 26
sale la venta [baynta] 61
sandals las sandalias [sandaleeas] 67
satisfied contento/-a [kontaynto/-a]
Saturday el sábado [sabado] 18
saucepan la olla [oya] 36
scheduled flight el vuelo de línea
    [vwaylo day leenaya] 30
scissors las tijeras [teekhayras] 61
sea urchin el erizo de mar [ayreetho
    day mar] 53
sea el mar [mar] 53
seafood los mariscos [mareeskos] 45
seasick mareado/-a
    [marayado/-a] 31, 73
season la estación [estatheeon] 18

seat el asiento [aseeaynto] 30, 31
second el segundo [saygoondo] 19
self-service el autoservicio
    [aootosayrbeetheeo] 40, 61
senior citizen la tercera edad
    [tayrthayra aydad] 29, 52
sentence la sentencia
    [sayntayntheea] 78
separate separado/-a [sayparado/-a]
series la fila [feela]
serious serio/-a [sayreeo/-a]
service el servicio [serveetheeo] 41
sex el sexo [sayxo]
shaver la máquina de afeitar
    [makeena day afayeetar] 68
shawl el chal [chal] 65
ship el barco [barko] 31
shirt la camisa [kameesa] 20, 65
shoe el zapato [thapato] 65, 67
shoelace los cordones de zapato
    [kordonays day thapato] 65
shoe shop la zapatería
    [thapatayreea] 61, 65
shop la tienda [teeaynda] 61
shopping, go ir de compras [eer day
    kompras] 36, 61
shop window el escaparate
    [ayskaparatay] 61
shore la orilla [oreelya] 53, 56
short corto/-a [korto/-a]
shorts los pantalones cortos
    [pantalonays kortos] 65
show (vb) mostrar [mostrar] 49
show el espectáculo
    [ayspayktakoolo] 12, 57
shower la ducha [doocha] 33, 36
sickness las náuseas [naoosayas] 75
side el lado [lado]
signature la firma [feerma] 21
signpost el indicador de camino
    [eendeekador day kameeno] 22
silk la seda [sayda] 65
single soltero/-a [soltayro/-a] 14
sister la hermana [ayrmana] 13
sister-in-law la cuñada [koonyada] 13
situation la situación [seetooatheeon]
skirt la falda [falda] 65
sky el cielo [theeaylo] 20
sleep (vb) dormir [dormeer] 32
sleeper car el coche-cama [kochay
    kama] 30
slim delgado/-a [daylgado/-a]
slow(-ly) lento/-a [laynto/-a]

small pequeño/-a [pay**kay**nyo/-a]
smell el olor [o**lor**]
snack la merienda [mayree**ayn**da] 40
soap el jabón [kha**bon**] 39, 71
socks los calcetines [kalthay**teen**ays] 65
soft blando/-a [**blan**do/-a]
sold out! ¡Agotado! [ago**tado**] 57
solicitor el/la abogado/-a
  [abo**gado**/-a] 79
son el hijo [**ee**kho] 13
sorry ¡Perdón! [payr**don**] 14
south el sur [soor] 22
special offer la oferta especial [o**fayr**ta
  ayspay**thee**al] 61
special rate la tarifa especial [ta**ree**fa
  ayspay**thee**al] 31
specialities las especialidades
  [ayspaytheealee**dad**ays] 40
spectacles las gafas [**gaf**as] 69, 70
speed la velocidad [vaylothee**dad**] 21
spoilt podrido/-a [po**dree**do/-a]
sponge la esponja [ays**pon**kha] 61
spoon la cuchara [koo**chara**] 43
sport el deporte [day**por**tay] 15, 54
sports jacket la chaqueta
  [cha**kay**ta] 65
sportsground el campo de deportes
  [**kam**po day day**por**tays] 39
spring la primavera [preema**bay**ra] 18
square (public) la plaza
  [**plath**a] 22, 51
staircase la escalera [ayska**lay**ra]
stamp el sello [**say**o] 61, 80
start principio [preenthee**pee**o] 54
state el estado [ays**tado**]
station la estación [aysta**thee**on] 28, 29
stationery la papelería
  [papaylay**ree**a] 64
stay the night pasar la noche [pa**sar**
  la **noch**ay]
stay la estancia [ays**tan**theea] 31
steep escarpado [ayskar**pado**]
stone la piedra [pee**ay**dra] 56
stop! ¡Alto! [**alto**]
stopover la escala [ays**kala**] 30
storey el piso [**pee**so] 32
storm la tempestad [taympays**tad**] 20, 55
story (literature) el cuento [**kwayn**to]
story (account) historia [hees**to**reea]
straight ahead derecho [day**raych**o]
street la calle [**ka**-yay] 22, 33
studio el taller [ta-**yayr**] 25
suburb el suburbio [soo**boor**beeo] 22

suede el ante [**an**tay] 65, 69
suit el traje [**trak**hay] 65
suitcase la maleta [ma**lay**ta] 21, 31
sum el importe [eem**por**tay] 40, 61
summer el verano [bay**rano**] 18
sun el sol [sol] 20
Sunday el domingo [do**meen**go] 18
sunglasses las gafas de sol [**gaf**as day
  sol] 70
sunlounger la tumbona [toom**bona**] 53
supermarket el supermercado
  [soopermayr**kado**] 36, 61
supper la cena [**thay**na] 18, 40
supplement el suplemento
  [sooplay**mayn**to]
surname el apellido [apay-**yee**do] 12
surprise la sorpresa [sor**pray**sa]
sweatshirt la sudadera
  [sooda**day**ra] 65
sweets los dulces [**dool**thays] 47
swim nadar [na**dar**] 53
swimming costume el traje de baño
  [**trak**hay day **ban**yo] 53, 67
swimming pool la piscina
  [pees**thee**na] 34, 53
swimming trunks el bañador
  [banya**dor**] 53, 67

T

table la mesa [**may**sa] 40
tablets las pastillas [pas**tee**yas] 76
take (vb) tomar [to**mar**]
take-off (aero) el despegue
  [days**pay**gay] 30
tampons los tampones [tam**pon**ays] 71
taxi el taxi [**tax**ee] 28, 35
telegram el telegrama [taylay**grama**] 80
telephone code el prefijo
  [pray**feek**ho] 82
telephone el teléfono [tay**lay**fono] 33, 82
temperature la temperatura
  [taympayra**too**ra] 20, 73
terminus la terminal [tayr**mee**nal] 29
terrible terrible [tay**ree**blay]
thank you gracias [**grath**eeas] 13, 14
theatre el teatro [tay**a**tro] 51, 57
theft el robo [**robo**] 78, 79
thick gordo/-a [**gordo**/-a]
thin delgado/-a [dayl**gado**/-a]
thing la cosa [**ko**sa]
thirst la sed [sayd] 48
this este/a [**ays**tay/-a]
Thursday el jueves [khway**bays**] 18

ticket el billete [beelyayte]
27, 28, 29, 57
tie (n) la corbata [korbata] 67
tights los leotardos [layotardos] 67
time (o'clock) la hora [ora] 17
time el tiempo [teeaympo] 17
timetable el horario [orareeo] 27, 29
timid tímido/-a [teemeedo/-a]
tip la propina [propeena] 83
tired cansado/-a [kansado/-a]
tiring fatigoso/-a [fateegoso/-a]
tobacco el tabaco [tabako] 70, 71
tobacconist el estanco [aystanko] 71
together juntos/-as [khoontos/-as]
toilet paper el papel higiénico [papayl
eekheeayneeko] 34, 71
toilets los aseos [asayos] 31, 83
tomorrow la mañana [manyana] 12, 19
toothbrush el cepillo de dientes
[thaypeeyo day deeayntays] 71
toothpaste la pasta dentífrica [pasta
daynteefreeka] 71
tour guide el/la guía [geea] 50
tourist office la oficina de turismo
[ofeetheena day tooreesmo] 49
tourist el/la turista [tooreesta] 21
towel la toalla [to-aya] 35, 39, 43
tower la torre [toray] 51
town (plan) (el plano de) la ciudad
[(plano day) la theeoodad] 39, 49
town hall el ayuntamiento
[ayoontameeaynto] 51
toy el juguete [khoogaytay] 61
traffic lights el semáforo
[saymaforo] 22
traffic el tráfico [trafeeko] 23
train el tren [trayn] 28–30
trainers las zapatillas de deporte
[thapateeyas day dayportay] 54
translate traducir [tradootheer] 78
travel agent la agencia de viajes
[akhayntheea day beeakhays] 49
traveller's cheque el cheque de viaje
[chaykay day beeakhay] 34, 77
tree el árbol [arbol] 56
trousers los pantalones
[pantalonays] 20
truck el camión [kameeon] 22
true verdadero [vayrdadayro]
T-shirt la camiseta [kameesayta] 65
Tuesday el martes [martays] 18
tunnel el túnel [toonayl] 22
tweezers las pinzas [peenthas] 71

typical típico/-a [teepeeko/-a] 69
tyre el neumático [nayoomateeko] 26

U
ugly feo/-a [fayo/-a]
umbrella el paraguas [paragooas] 61
uncle el tío [teeo] 13
underwear (gents') los calzoncillos
[kalthontheeyos] 67
underwear (ladies') las bragas
[bragas] 67
unhappy desgraciado/-a
[daysgratheeado/-a]/ infeliz
[eenfeleeth]
unknown desconocido/-a
[dayskonotheedo/-a]
urgent urgente [oorkhayntay] 72

V
valid válido [valeedo] 21, 27
various diferente [deefayrayntay]
vegetables las verduras
[bayrdooras] 47, 62
vest la camiseta [kameesayta] 65
vet el veterinario [vaytayreenareeo]
video cassette la casete de vídeo
[kasaytay day veedayo] 68
view la vista [veesta] 51
village la aldea [aldaya] le pueblecito
[pwayblaytheeto] 22
visa el visado [veesado] 21
visit la visita [veeseeta] 49

W
waistcoat el chaleco [chalayko] 67
wait (vb) esperar [ayspayrar]
waiter el camarero [kamarayro] 41
waitress la camarera [kamarayra] 41
waiting room la sala de espera [sala
day ayspayra] 72
walk el paseo [pasayo] 49
wallet la cartera [kartayra] 78
want (vb) querer [kayrayr]
warm caliente [kaleeayntay] 20, 40
wash (vb) lavar [lavar] 36, 67
washing powder el detergente
[daytayrkhayntay] 71
water el agua (f) [agua] 36, 39
wave la ola [ola] 55
weather forecast la previsión del
tiempo [prayveeseeon del teeaympo] 19
weather el tiempo [teeaympo] 19
wedding la boda [boda]

Wednesday el miércoles [meeayrkolays] 18
week la semana [saymana] 15, 18
weekdays los días laborables [los deeas laborablays] 18
weigh pesar [paysar] 19
weight el peso [payso] 61
welcome! ¡Bienvenido(s)! [beeaynvayneedo(s)]
west el oeste [ooaystay] 22
wet mojado/-a [mokhado/-a]
white blanco [blanko] 20
Whitsunstide Pentecostés [payntaykostays] 14, 60
wife la esposa [aysposa] 13
wind el viento [beeaynto] 20
winter el invierno [eenbeeayrno] 18
wish (vb) desear [daysayar]
witness el/la testigo [taysteego] 27

wood (firewood) la leña [laynya] 36
wood la madera [madayra]
woodland el bosque [boskay] 51
wool la lana [lana] 65
word la palabra [palabra] 80
work el trabajo [trabakho]
world el mundo [moondo]
wrong falso/-a [falso/-a]

Y
year el año [anyo] 19
yes sí [see]
young jóven [khobayn]
youth hostel el albergue juvenil [albayrgay khoobayneel] 38

Z
zip la cremallera [kraymayayra] 61

Spanish–English A–Z

A
abierto open
a. C. (antes de Cristo) before Christ (BC)
acceso access
¡Adelante! Come in!
aduana border, customs
aeropuerto airport
agencia de viajes travel agency
agotado sold out
aire acondicionado air conditioning
alarma emergency brake
albergue juvenil youth hostel
almuerzo lunch
alquiler de bicicletas cycle hire
alquiler de coches car hire
ambulancia ambulance
andén platform
aparcamiento (vigilado) (supervised) car-park
aseos toilets
atasco traffic jam
¡Atención! Warning!
autopista motorway
autoservicio self-service

autovía expressway
AVE (Alta Velocidad Española) Spanish high speed train
ayuntamiento town hall

B
banco bank
biblioteca library
bicicleta bicycle
¡Bienvenido! Welcome!
billete ticket
bomberos fire brigade
buzón letter box

C
Caballeros gents' toilet
caja till
caja de ahorros savings bank
caliente warm
calle street
callejón sin salida cul-de-sac
cambio bureau de change
carné de identidad identity card/passport
carnicería butchers

carretera main road
carta menu
cartas letters
¡Ceda el paso! Give way!
cena evening meal
centro centre
cepo wheel-clamp
cerrado closed
¡Cerrar la puerta! Close the door!
comestibles food shop
Compañia (Cía.) company (Co.)
consigna left luggage
correos post
corrida (de toros) bullfighting
Cortes Spanish parliament
cruce junction
cuartos room
¡Cuidado! Warning!
CV (caballo de vapor) horsepower
   (BHP)

D
d. C. (después de Cristo) (Anno
   domini) AD
desvío diversion
dirección address
disco de estacionamiento parking
   disc
domingo Sunday

E
¡Empuje! Press!
entrada entrance, entrance ticket
entrada libre free admission
estación station
estado civil marital status
estanco tobacconist
estropeado faulty
expo(sición) exhibition
extintor fire extinguisher

F
festivo holiday
fiesta festival
firma signature
frío cold
fuego fire
fumadores smokers

G
gasolina petrol
giro obligatorio roundabout
gratuito free

grúa tow-away truck
Guardia Civil Spanish civil guard
   (police)

H
hecho a mano hand-made
Hermanos (Hnos.) brothers

I
iglesia church
impuesto sobre valor añadido (IVA)
   VAT
incluído included
información information

L
lavabos toilets
lavado en seco dry cleaning
lavandería laundry
libre free
librería bookshop
lista de correos poste restante
llegada arrival

M
mayores adults
miércoles Wednesday
misa church mass
monedas coins, change

N
no fumadores non-smokers
noche night

O
ocupado occupied
oficina de turismo tourist
   information

P
página (pag.) page
panadería bakery
parada bus stop
paso de peatones pedestrian crossing
¡Peligro de muerte! Serious danger!
peluquería hairdressers
pescadería fishmongers
piscina swimming pool
plato del día dish of the day
playa beach
plaza de toros bull ring
policía police
¡Precaución! Warning!

privado private (no entry)
¡Prohibida la entrada! No entry!
¡Prohibido el paso! No through road!
¡Prohibido fumar! No smoking!
pesetas (ptas.) pesetas

R

rebajas bargains
recepción reception
reducción reduction
RENFE (Red Nacional de Ferrocarriles
  Españoles) Spanish railway company
residente en resident in
retraso delay

S

salida de emergencia emergency exit
se alquila for hire
se vende for sale
sellos stamps
Señoras ladies (toilets)
sentido único one-way street
servicio incluído service included
servicios toilets
Sociedad Anónima (S.A.) Limited
  company (Ltd)
sin plomo lead-free
¡Socorro! Help!
sr. (señor) Mr
sra. (señora) Mrs

srta. (señorita) Miss
supermercado supermarket
suplemento supplement

T

tabacos tobacco goods
TAV (Tren de Alta Velocidad) high-
  speed train
Telefónica Spanish telephone
  company
temporada (alta) (high) season
tercera edad senior citizens
¡Tire! Pull!

U

UE (Unidad Europea) European
  Union (EU)

V

válido valid
venta anticipada advanced sales
verbena public festival
vía platform
visita guiada guided tour
vuelo doméstico domestic flight
vuelo internacional international
  flight